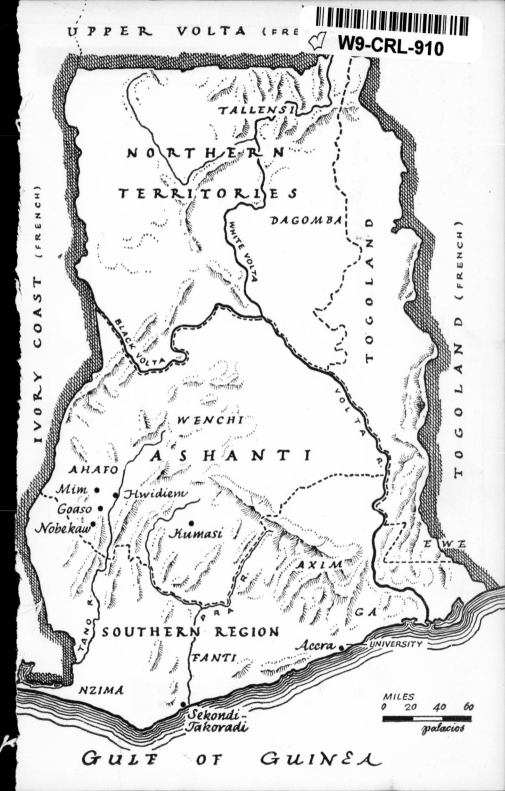

UPPER VOLTA (FRE

IVORY COAST (FRENCH)

TALLENSI

NORTHERN

TERRITORIES

DAGOMBA

WHITE VOLTA

BLACK VOLTA

TOGOLAND (FRENCH)

TOGOLAND (FRENCH)

WENCHI

ASHANTI

AHAFO

Mim

Goaso

Nobekaw

Hwidiem

Kumasi

VOLTA R.

EWE

AXIM

GA

TANO R.

PRA R.

SOUTHERN REGION

FANTI

Accra

UNIVERSITY

NZIMA

Sekondi-Takoradi

MILES

0   20   40   60

palacios

GULF   OF   GUINEA

ROBERT A. LYSTAD

THE ASHANTI

A Proud People

Rutgers University Press
New Brunswick · New Jersey

Endpaper maps by Rafael Palacios

To My Wife

Author's Note

The research on which this book is based was conducted in 1949-50 under a fellowship granted by the Social Science Research Council of New York. Professor Melville J. Herskovits, Director of the Africa Studies Program of Northwestern University, stimulated the initial interest in this research and has continued to be a source of ideas and insight into African cultures. Although the materials and the interpretations are those of the author, he has also benefited from the published works of other students of Ashanti and West Africa, particularly those of the late Captain R. S. Rattray, whose books on Ashanti may be regarded as "the classics," Professor Meyer Fortes, of Cambridge University, and Professor Kofi S. Busia, of the University College of Ghana.

In the field the author enjoyed the expert services of Mr. Charles E. Donkoh, of Wenchi, Ashanti; he was an able interpreter of the language and culture which are his own. Nana Kwami Nkwantabisa, the town chief, and the citizens of Goaso, too numerous to mention individually, received the author, quizzically at first, but with traditional hospitality and with a degree of acceptance and co-operation which a stranger could hardly have expected. And in a cultural and historical sense, the ancestors of modern Ashanti, through their representative, Nana Otumfuo Sir Osei Agyeman Prempeh II, Asantehene, have contributed greatly to this study.

Contents

1. Of Africa and Africans   3

2. The Deep Roots   13

3. Their Native Land   24

4. Meet My Families   44

5. Learning to Live   73

6. Matters of Life and Death   87

7. Democracy, Old and New   104

8. Money Grows on Trees   131

9. The Wider World   154

10. The Future World   187

Index   207

p 95

THE ASHANTI: *A Proud People*

1. Of Africa and Africans

Africa fascinates world-conscious Americans for various reasons. One is political. Both fortunately and unfortunately, Africa is an important base for military operations in a world war; its growing populations are likely to become implicated in the battle between the two major political ideologies of our time. It is involved in some of the most explosive of contemporary social conflicts; words like Mau-Mau and apartheid are heard around the world. But above all, it is fascinating because the emergence of new nations and the sound of new voices in an old land excite the hopes of all who believe in the right and eventual ability of men to determine their own course.

Another sphere of interest is economic. The extent of the role which Africa played in the development of European and American economies during the eighteenth century and in the creation and maintenance of at least a kind of political and economic power balance in the nineteenth century is often underestimated. It was a major, if largely involuntary, contribution. Today Africa produces large quantities of vegetable oils, coffee, sisal, and other agricultural products, much of the world's supply of gold, diamonds, uranium, lead, manganese, and other crucial metals, and—of special importance to this book—more than half the world's supply of cocoa. Africans buy things, too, and the economic development of the continent provides employment and prosperity for many thousands of European and American workers and entrepreneurs. Its economic potential has not yet been fully explored and, though the old colonial dreams of untold resources, swarms of cheap labor, and insatiable markets have largely evaporated in the bright sun of economic reality, Africa's unknown quantities still lure the hardier risk takers.

The enticements of adventure, of big game and exotic sights, sounds, and smells attract the hardier, well-financed spender—who wants to feel like a risk taker—or the would-be-free frontiersman to Africa for lion tails, for elephant tusks, for antelope heads and skins. The missionary too goes to Africa—to seek out the lost, sometimes with Bible, holy sacrament, and testimony foremost, often with hoe and good seeds, with drugs, syringe, and scalpel, or with textbook breaking the way through what he supposes to be the heathen jungle. And then there is the anthropologist or other social scientist or anyone fascinated by human beings and their activities; these are attracted to Africa by the hope that they can satisfy a restless curiosity about ways of life different from their own; or they are driven to Africa in the attempt to shed some small light upon the greatest problem raised in any generation—the problem of why men think and act the way they do.

Africa holds its fascinations and satisfactions for all these—and for others, whatever their motives for looking at this remarkable, still little-known world within our world. The author of this book is concerned as an anthropologist with African people and their behavior. Living with Africans and trying to learn a little of what it is like to be an African is, he feels, the best road to enjoyment in Africa, but it is certainly not the only one, for Africa holds many and varied satisfactions.

In a certain sense this book is about people in general rather than about Africa. It concerns a few people, but a few can reveal a great deal about many others. Since these people are Africans, what they say and do can at least be taken as a clue to the sayings and doings of many more people, especially of Africans, but of all others as well, including Americans.

Anthropologists generally, though not always, interest themselves in a relatively small group of people whom they wish to get to know very well. This book adopts such an approach for two reasons: first, because most of the current books about Africa—other than very specialized books—deal in sweeping terms with the whole continent or at the very least with a nation. They tend, too, to analyze political events, the dramatic surgings and tensions which come to focus in the realm of national political institutions, in the heady, heroic atmosphere of the great leader, or in the bloody, brutal atmosphere of racial or anti-imperial conflict, actual or potential. If the people come into view, they are seen, somehow, as if out of focus, colorful, quaint, queer, savage, irresponsible, childlike, incomprehensible, but seldom in clear perspective, with their orderly, predictable patterns of living, patterns which, on the whole, provide each individual with his own security and satisfactions and his group with dignity and integrity. This book, then, seeks to supplement the books which give a hasty glance at many things and many places with a rounded, though not complete, look at a few things in a relatively small place.

The second reason for adopting such an approach is that

5

the people whose life is here introduced are, in numerous respects, typical people. Most Africans are country people, living close to the land and loving the land. If the headlines
are made in the cities, the nation is made in the country—
in the small towns, the villages, and the hamlets which comprise what in Africa is called "the bush." If the people who
appear to wield the power live in the cities, it is the people
in the country who must ultimately accept their authority—
or reject it. They are the people who produce the wealth,
for consumption and for export, and they cannot be dismissed with a few sentences. They deserve to be seen, to be
understood.

The claim of "typicality" cannot, of course, be made without some reservations, for Africa is a huge continent with
highly diversified terrain, climate, and societies. No single volume can presume to tell all about Africa, and no single small
group of people mirrors all the complexities of African ways
of life. The diversities of two hundred years ago, before the
heavy impact of European societies began to be felt, have
been compounded during the past fifty years by contact of
varying degrees of intensity with Europeans, and the eddies
and crosscurrents of cultural change dismay the observer
who wishes to make sense out of it all and to derive some
permanent conclusions about it. Yet if a start is to be made,
the country is a good place in which to make it. Its people
are as typical as can be found; there are many, many like
them. If in the country it is impossible to learn everything
about everyone, at least it is possible to learn a few things
well.

The Ashanti are predominantly just such a country people,
creating their livelihood and their proud culture out of the

6

African soil. They constitute a small though important and increasingly well-known segment of those millions of people who live in West Africa. This name has been given to all that territory lying between the Atlantic Ocean at Dakar, the city at the westernmost outreach of the continent, and Equatorial Africa, where the east-west line of the coast dips southward to cross the equator.

West Africa unrolls in a more than 3,000-mile long, green carpet of a gently undulating tropical rain forest. To the south the sand beaches endlessly advance and recede under the monotonous surf of the Atlantic Ocean, long a barrier to contact with the rest of the world. Two hundred miles inland from the coast the forest zone quite suddenly becomes a flat, wooded grassland stretching northward to merge with the enormous wastes of the Sahara Desert. The desert has not been quite so effective a barrier as the ocean, but it has hardly encouraged the rapid or frequent exchange of ideas or things or people. To the east the forest and the grassland roll on across many hard, isolating miles to the varied topography of East Africa.

Not far from the midpoint of the long, smooth coastline, which roughly parallels the equator just a few degrees to the south, is the nation called Ghana, If this name is less than familiar, it is probably because of its newness, for the nation to which it has been given is hardly more than fifty years old, and during all of those years, up to 1957, it was called the Gold Coast, British West Africa. The new name, adopted in 1957, signifies, among other things, a change in status from a British colony to an independent, self-governing member of the British Commonwealth of Nations.

Ghana, as was the Gold Coast before it, is subdivided politically into four major areas, the central one of which is called

7

Ashanti. And the people of this central state are called the Ashanti. They are the people of this book, and in them may be seen something of the dignity and humanity of most of the world's people.

Before approaching West Africa, Ghana, and Ashanti directly for a closer view of their history and way of life it may be useful to cast at least a glance at the physical appearance of the West Africans, briefly to consider the implications of their racial heritage for their cultural heritage, and finally to distinguish them from other Africans with whom they may easily have become confused.

In appearance West Africans closely resemble scores of millions of Africans who inhabit the continent all the way from the Sahara Desert to the Cape of Good Hope at its southernmost point, and if the term "race" signified no more than a cluster of frequently observed, genetically inherited physical characteristics, it would suffice simply to state that they are members of that subdivision of the Negroid race called the Forest Negro. In the thinking of many persons, however, racial characteristics have been forced to carry connotations for which they are in no way qualified. They have been made to serve as a causal explanation of the behavior of a group of persons who carry these physical characteristics, behavior which is rightfully attributable only to historical conditions and events.

The classification of West Africans and most other Africans as Negroid simply means that certain inherited physical characteristics occur with greater frequency among the peoples occupying this part of Africa than they do among peoples in most other parts of the world. These differences are conspicuous even to the person who looks only casually at physical similarities and differences. What is less widely recognized, however, is that these differences are few in number when compared to the similarities between the races. The two other major racial divisions of the world's people are the Mongoloid and the Caucasoid; the former includes most Asiatics and American Indians, the latter includes those people generally called "whites," whose recent racial origins are in Europe, northern Africa, western Asia, and India. So like each other are all the members of all these races that the specialists who classify animals according to their similarities and differences call all by a single name, *homo sapiens*.

When human beings, like plants or animals, are members of the same species, any apparent differences between them are probably so slight as to be irrelevant to the survival or biological fitness of the species. A member of any one of the races may not care to have his daughter mate with a member of any other race because of the social position it has come to occupy, but biologically there can be no objection to it. The obviousness of these differences is responsible for the way in which they have tended to overshadow the overwhelming number of similarities.

Another often-overlooked characteristic of each of the races is the astonishing range of variation in physical features to be found within any single race. Just as the Caucasoid classification includes fair-skinned, blond-haired, blue-eyed Nordics along with olive- or even brown-skinned, black-haired, brown-eyed Mediterraneans, so does the Negroid classification embrace a considerable number of groups which would never be mistaken for one another. The tallest human group in the world, the Nilotics, who average about six feet in height, are Negroid; the smallest human group in the world, the Pygmies, averaging under five feet in height, are Negroid. And

9

between these extremes are most Negroids; their average height is about the same as that of Caucasoids.

As for that elusive, hard-to-measure quality called intelligence and that equally baffling capacity to achieve a worthwhile culture, social and psychological research has uncovered few differences in performance between racial groups which cannot be satisfactorily explained on grounds other than differences in inherited intelligence or differences in inherent ability to create a culture. The crucial factors on which differences hinge may be best described as environmental, either human or nonhuman, social or physical.

The consensus of the social sciences, simply stated, is that in any racial group the intelligence of normal people, who always comprise the vast majority, will range from dull to bright; at either end of the scale will be found a few persons who are either too dull for words or too bright for words. Some of these differences within a race can undoubtedly be traced to inherited characteristics, but for most of the people most of the differences can be accounted for by differences in the learning and living situations or by the nature of the intelligence tests themselves. Social scientists have not yet solved the problem of devising tests which actually measure this vague, ill-defined something-or-other called "intelligence." The results of the tests they do use certainly flatter no one group over another, least of all the huge, motley, mixed-up group of people called a race. The last word has yet to be uttered on intelligence or cultural achievement, but enough has been learned to persuade social scientists to stop looking for inherent mental differences between the races; the factors they now analyze include race only as one of several social, environmental variables, not as a biological, inherited variable.

The photograph of an Ashanti politician performing his

official duties shows something of the perplexed, responsible expression of an American stockbroker who has sold ten thousand shares an hour too late. As the chief of a town which is petitioning the government to construct a road in its direction he might well be mulling over a foolproof scheme for persuading his citizens to raise the tax millage to pay for it. If his problem does not appear to be a typically African problem, neither does he present a typically African countenance. Yet people who resemble him physically and have problems as knotty as his—or far knottier—are to be found throughout West Africa, and the faces of these men and the problems they are solving suggest only in small degree the wide variations from the stereotype which are to be found on this continent.

West Africa is not the land of King Solomon's mines, nor of big game safaris. The nearest approximations to such fabulous regions are either several thousands of miles to the east—there are at least safaris there—or more thousands of miles to the west in Hollywood. The Mau-Mau, with its real grievances and its unreal, magical, terroristic solutions, is likewise far away in East Africa, although far milder expressions of resentment against Europeans are voiced in West Africa. The beds of glistening diamonds and the enormous veins of gold, the native reservations and the apartheid—racial segregation—problems of South Africa lie far away to the southeast. North Africa's bazaars and bitter agitation for release from European control are separated from West Africa by the Sahara Desert wastes. The inscrutable sphinx, the ancient tombs, and the tragic, modern dilemmas of Egypt and the rest of the Arab world are equally distant. The independent republic of Liberia lies within West Africa, but neither it nor the Americo-Liberians who control it are representative of the area. Nor is Ethiopia, the only other African territory to avoid extensive foreign political domination, typical of this region. The Belgian Congo, administered in an orderly, paternalistic fashion by benevolent but wary Europeans, is distinctive in its own way. West Africa is none of these.

If the traveler is searching for grand scenery, for exotic discoveries, or for crackling adventure, he should look elsewhere. The elephants, the lions, the leopards have long since left West Africa for more hospitable areas. The midnight orgies of glistening, naked savages leaping around blazing fires never existed here—as they never did anywhere in the uncomprehending fashion of cartoons and storybooks. Farmers who rise with the sun retire soon after it sets, and the normal West African night in the country resounds to nothing more pulse-quickening than the occasional racket of crickets, the crackle of cooling, contracting, corrugated metal, and the boomp and skitter of nuts and twigs rolling down an inclined tin roof. Now and then the early evening—occasionally an entire night—may be punctuated by the exciting, polyrhythmic rattle of dancing drums, but most nights are still and sleepy.

West Africa is not quite peculiarly itself and different from other areas of Africa and of the world. The reasons why it is unique and at the same time similar to the rest of the world are to be found in its history—in the conditions and events of the recent past and, so far as evidence permits, the distant past, and equally in the conditions and events of the present day.

2. The Deep Roots

The continent of Africa, of which Ashanti is a minute part, is gradually becoming less murky a place than it has always been for everyone, including Africans, but those shadowy mists are not quickly dispelled. If notions of what Africa is or is not are still hazy, it is due in part to the sub-Sahara's lack of co-operation in making itself known. It has been relatively isolated and inaccessible, surrounded by seas and desert. Nonliterate, it has lived its past without written records, and the recency of serious world interest in Africa has left the larger part of its history unremembered and unobserved by those who could have recorded it.

Even now those African languages which are written do not have an extensive literature. It is not that the languages themselves are deficient in any respect; they are indeed as capable as any other sound-bound, concept-bound language of communicating what people have to say. It is just that symbolizing with written marks rather than with spoken sounds never took hold in much of Africa south of the Sahara until the Europeans introduced it, and it is still the European languages, English, French, German, Portuguese, Spanish and Afrikaans (a Dutch dialect spoken in South Africa) that make up the bulk of written literature.

Because of the lack of written records, African tribal history consists largely of what people remember, and memory can be a pleasantly selective agent carrying back only to the better things of the last few generations within one's own group. At the same time, the supposed social inferiority of other groups can be perpetuated and reinforced by the same selective memories. History can easily be warped by advantage seekers, and unwritten history is especially vulnerable in this respect. At no time is this more the case than when contemporary individuals are closely identified with social groups which in time past have had some stigma attached to them, stigma like defeat or capture in war, or traditions of frequent witchcraft or financial indebtedness. Many such groups in Africa, families, clans, tribes, like minority groups in any society, thus find themselves inheritors of a poor social position through no fault of their own and for reasons locked in a hazy past.

For more than a thousand years North African Moslems have written sketchily about West African history and, during the past five hundred years, more and more Europeans have been recording their observations and interpretations. But Africa is a large place and for many areas and peoples there is only a patchwork of knowledge about events prior to a century or less ago. The best-informed persons—outside of Africans themselves, who are likely to know the history of the last few generations in their own vicinity—are the anthropologists and historians, and their knowledge is incomplete. What they are able to do is to piece together, from such esoteric material as folklore, art, beliefs, social customs and institutions, group relationships, archaeological findings, and from the uncertain, recent written records, reconstructions of what might have happened on a very general, sweeping scale, and their accounts are necessarily prefaced with "perhaps," "possibly," and "maybe."

The history of West Africa can be recounted only in some such general terms. During the past fifteen hundred years or so, expanding empires or states in the grassland areas of the Sudan to the north forced certain groups to migrate into the forest region, where they met with still more ancient inhabitants or with other groups moving westward along the coast from points to the east. Before that are perhaps migrations following a westerly course through the grassland belt which stretches across the continent, and back of them there is only silence. The source of the Negro populations of the world has not been determined; Africa itself or southern Asia may have produced this particular one of the world's three major racial groups and cradled at least part of its culture.

When, in the fifteenth, sixteenth, and seventeenth centuries, the European mercantilists began to explore West African potentialities as a source of raw materials and labor and as a market for expanding production they found numerous groups of similar but apparently unrelated peoples. By the time of the great European colonial partition late in the nineteenth century something more had been learned of the area and its people, and since then many, though by no means all, of the gaps have been filled in.

The peoples of this region spoke—and still speak—more than a hundred different languages, many of them used by only a few thousand people, although all of them are about as closely related as is English to German or Dutch or to French or to Russian. The peoples of the forest zone of West Africa were similar, too, in the ways in which they made their livelihood, for nearly all were—and still are—country people, gardeners of such domesticated food crops as yams, cocoyams, oil palm, and plantain, banana and other fruits, and breeders of goats and fowl. Cattle and other larger livestock could not be raised in the tsetse fly infested forest zone, although they were raised in the northern grasslands. Tools were constructed of stone and wood or, where available, iron; clothing was of bark or of woven raffia. In many areas regularized, orderly markets conducted a lively sale of surplus production, with money—cowrie shells, gold dust, salt, or other items—as the medium of exchange. Skilled wood carvers and metalworkers in gold, iron, and later brass and bronze created artistic pieces for utilitarian, decorative, or religious and magical purposes, works of art whose conception and style came, in recent times, to be admired by numerous European and American artists.

Social life centered primarily in the family (though it was an extensive family) and in the local community, which comprised a number of such kin groups. Polygyny was universally desired, although undoubtedly most men failed to achieve the ideal, and firmly established codes regulated relationships between the sexes and their families. Occasionally several communities were linked by marriage or by kinship, and a rather loose political system marked by popular checks on the rulers was devised. The rulers themselves were usually selected from royal families, and they functioned to maintain social order within the communities and to establish connections with neighboring groups. Feuds and raiding often interrupted the otherwise peaceful coexistence of the various communities, whose normal exchange was that of trade, marriage partners, and ideas. In some areas male secret societies, some of them with female counterparts, were organized for mutual aid, social control, and sometimes for nefarious purposes like blackmail.

Outside the class confines of royalty and commoner were the lowliest of the slaves, enemies or recently captured prisoners of war, persons whose rights were severely limited. But within the social class confines, if on the lowest level, were those older slaves or descendants of slaves whose rights were considerable and whose treatment was generous, including freedom of marriage to free men or women, some personal mobility, property ownership, and justice. To be a slave was not precisely to be free, but neither was it a hopeless condition; indeed, some lowly free men might have preferred slavery of this limited sort.

Participating in the affairs of men were the ancestors, those founders, real or mythical, remembered or imaginatively reconstructed, who displayed a lively and effective interest in their descendants. These formed the central theological and ritual core of West African religion, although they were augmented by beliefs in gods—sometimes many of them—who also took a hand in maintaining a proper relationship between men and between men and their universe. Together ancestors and gods provided a sufficient reason for behavior according to the well-developed, formalized rules and a fearsome punishment for being antisocial. They also provided the occasion for the development of specially skilled, professional workers in religion and magic, who applied their revealed knowledge to the cure of people's ills and problems and to reducing the dangers abroad in the world.

At several centers in the forest zone during the five centuries after the first appearance of the Europeans, political developments of a complex sort were occurring. Perhaps stimulated by the progressive rise of empires over a period of nearly a thousand years in the grassland areas to the north—one of these was called Ghana—or by the gradual penetration of migrants from the north into the forests, a number of confederations and budding empires assumed shape beginning in the fourteenth century. Several of these reached their zeniths during the nineteenth century, when they were cut short or drastically changed by the arrival in force of the European powers. Elaborate state organizations, with decentralized but pyramiding bureaucracies and presided over by a sacred chief, flourished in at least four areas in the forests of West Africa.

Ashanti, founded at the beginning of the eighteenth century, was one of these. Lavish courtly dress, etiquette, and rituals glorified the politicians at successive hierarchical levels of organization; court systems, complete with chief judges, lawyers, and formalized legal codes set down in precedents and remembered in proverbs and often clarified by under-the-table payments, dispensed justice; effective tax systems collected wealth from the taxpayers, great and small; semipermanent military organizations extended the boundaries of the state and maintained internal order; the arts flourished, and specialists in many crafts created articles of trade for sale over wide areas. Contributing to the treasuries and the military power necessary for supporting such aspiring empires was the slave trade with the Europeans, who eagerly exchanged guns and the materials of a higher standard of living for the human laborers to be profitably sold to the plantations in the New World. This, in brief, is the West Africa into which, in the latter half of the nineteenth century, the Europeans launched their own imperial campaigns.

On a political map of West Africa the long east-west forest and grassland zones are cut by pink and yellow lines running north and south to indicate where, less than a hundred years ago, several European countries raced each other to establish their dominions and then to protect their dominions from encroachment from beyond the pink and yellow lines they had painted on the map. It did not matter then that those lines bisected groups of people whose natural and cultural affiliations were with each other through identical ways of life and, in many cases, even through bonds of kinship. That did not matter then; only the lines and the deceptively rich promises they enclosed mattered, and the little colored lines, once drawn, could be altered only by big diplomatic conferences around big bartering tables in Europe or by a big world war. It is only now that Africans are beginning to draw and, in some cases, redraw their own boundaries.

The land between two of these lines—pink ones—came to be known as the Gold Coast, British West Africa. Immediately to the west—yellow lines this time—the land came to be called the Ivory Coast, French West Africa. For several centuries the ships of Europe had called at stations along the West Coast to pick up their valuable cargoes, gold, ivory, and human slaves, and the names of the first two commodities remained to designate these lands. They remained, that is, until March, 1957, when the Gold Coast became free and independent Ghana, in proud recollection of one of the first of those ancient empires which had dominated a large territory in the grasslands of western Africa and given impetus, if indirectly, to the creation of the successful states within the forest region.

To the east is Togoland, a narrow territory which, prior to the arrival of the Europeans, belonged to several small, independent African societies. Some eighty years ago it became part of the German Empire; then, after World War I, it was divided into two narrower segments, one to be administered by the British and the other by the French under the League of Nations; next, after World War II, it was administered by the same two nations under the trusteeship terms of the United Nations. Now, by popular self-choice, the British section has joined itself to Ghana; the French section has declared itself for self-government within the French Union.

Ghana, for all the splendor of its past and the exciting but sobering prospect of its future, never has been exactly a tropical paradise, for such fabulous places exist only in fables. Between the northern and the central and southern sections there exist rather considerable differences of physical environment and of history and culture, and between the central and southern sections narrow differences within the broad similarities of culture have combined to maintain a measure of disunity between the peoples of even this small area. This disunity is reflected today in the division of Ghana into three major states in addition to Togoland.

The nation's approximately 4,500,000 inhabitants—all but a few thousand of them African—occupy a territory of about 105,000 square miles—a little more than twice the size of the state of New York. The slightly more than a million people of the northern territories live wholly within the grassland area, enduring the deflected hot breath of the Sahara Desert and toiling with difficulty to scratch an existence from the unco-operative land, while enjoying somewhat more success in the raising of cattle. Politically, most of them are organized into small groups, some of them under the domination of several aristocratic societies, others remaining independent in the marginal areas. Strongly influenced by Islam in their history and outlook, they feel more at home with similar peoples to the north and east than they do with the people of Ghana to the south.

The more than three million people in the central and southern states, Ashanti and the Gold Coast Colony, are almost wholly within the forest or the more temperate coastal regions. Closely bound by the ties of their common Akan language and culture, they have nevertheless been divided politically by the establishment of separate political states with special local traditions. Each of these states, despite its similarity to the others, has carefully and proudly attempted to preserve its own identity. Only in Ashanti did any considerable number of these small states give over a measure of their autonomy to a central confederation of states. Were this multiplication of local political interests and histories not enough to create disunity in Ghana, the people of the southeastern section of the country have closer historical affinity to the peoples of Dahomey and Nigeria, countries which lie farther to the east. The political boundaries established by the European competitors were certainly drawn with little regard for African patterns of unity or discord.

Artificial may be the word for Ghana, but it is not the only word. For striking through the regional differences there remain the numerous and penetrating similarities of many centuries. Added to these have been the more or less unified efforts of the colonial administration over half a century—over a full century in the southern colony of Ghana—and the spreading standardization of a way of life lived increasingly under modern conditions. The prospects of incorporating all these people into a single nation are not necessarily bleak.

Here is a way of life changing rapidly; here is a new nation arisen in the world. From closely knit societies—even including the more complicated Ashanti—in which the individual recognized his own worth largely in terms of traditional family and narrow community patterns there is gradually emerging a single society which provides him with less security but more varied opportunities through which he can find himself. The ideas, institutions, and machines of another part of the world are opening new avenues to personal expression and satisfaction. Everywhere there is the uncertainty about the old truths and the questioning of the new ones. This is disturbing to the questioner, disturbing to those who do not or cannot ask new questions about old things, disturbing to those who accept the old answers. There are more opportunities for the individual to become lost in the confusion of change. But here is real excitement, the excitement of human growth.

This nation, unlike the United States, has been born with a minimum of violence and a maximum of restraint. Some violence there is, but not so much as to create the fear of a holocaust. The costly, terrific tensions of racial strife have affected neither little girls nor their parents in Ashanti to any disturbing degree; the complex issues and gloomy prospects which divide the children of various races in East and South Africa have not arisen alarmingly in Ghana nor in any part of West Africa and, despite a degree of political and economic unrest, they are not likely to do so.

The African leaders of Ghana are confident that they have the maturity and the skill to carry through this birth and to minimize the trauma, and most Africans share this confidence. On a smaller, tribal scale they governed themselves in a kind of democratic manner for centuries. This background, together with the accumulative experience of more than fifty years of British administration, has, they are convinced, fitted them for national self-government. The centrifugal, parochial pull of the pre-European political groupings may leave the

national unity temporarily in doubt, and the economic under-
pinning of a country with grand pretensions may be thin
and spindly, but in time the nation should live well.

The British, though with considerable and perhaps understandable reluctance, have acknowledged the right to self-
government and at least the strong possibility of success for
such a nation. Having affirmed this right almost from the
outset of their rule in 1830, and having been propelled down
the logical road of their affirmation by the increasing pressure of vast African majorities who demanded the right to
exercise their rights, the British have, in rapid order over a
period of more than two decades, relinquished the degree of
their control. Now, in the year of Nyame (en-yah-may), the
creator-god, 1957, the Africans of Ghana are self-governing.
Now Ghana has an equal political status with Canada, Aus-
tralia, and the other respected members of the British Commonwealth of Nations.

3. Their Native Land

An agile witch or a roaming soul—many Ashanti firmly believe in both—could traverse the 125 miles from the Atlantic coast to central Ashanti in an easy, direct, night flight, but ordinary mortals wishing to go there must take a more circuitous route. One reason for this is Africa's nearly harborless coastline. Its shore, for short stretches, is attractive enough, lined as it is with sandy beaches and languid, stately palms. But the white-foamed surf washes restlessly at the unvarying, unindented rim of the continent, frustrating both those who want to enter and those who want to leave.

Of the two major ports of entry into Ghana at the present time, Sekondi-Takoradi provides the better landing facilities; its artificially constructed harbor carries the bulk of agricultural exports from the country. But Accra, a city of 175,000, capital of Ghana, provides the ship-to-shore passenger with more suspenseful drama, for here his ship heaves to about a mile from shore and awaits the arrival of the oversized rowboats which lighten the cargo, human and nonhuman, onto the beach. When the boats have bobbed up to the ship and the passenger has sucked in his breath, he is flung over the side in a rope-bound chair and lowered swiftly and decisively into the boat, which lurches upward on the crest of the swell to give him a jarring welcome to Ghana. Then he is off toward the shore, propelled cleanly through the rolling surf by the muscular, deep-bronze backs and arms and the plunging paddles of ten or twelve immigrant, seagoing stevedores from Liberia, the "Kru boys."

Among the thousands of dollars' worth of goods which have got to within 300 feet of their African destination—250 feet out from shore and 50 feet below the surface of the water— lies at least one Buick, pitched off the heaving deck joining two boats. But for each load lost overboard a sufficient number reach the beach, and the inefficient system will continue to operate until the new port some miles down the coast at Tema is completed.

Much more efficient, though hardly as exciting, is the arrival by plane, which touches down at the huge Accra airport just thirty-four hours after leaving New York. This prosaic journey comes to an end as the plane circles low over the green park and golf course and the white and pastel buildings of the University College of Ghana and settles to rest before the Lisbon Hotel and the Pan American Airways office building.

This, however, is not quite the Africa of Goaso, the town of this book, which is separated from Accra by 250 miles of road and by analogous cultural distances. To reach Goaso, far out in western Ashanti, it is necessary first to get to Kumasi, the capital of Ashanti. Of the various forms of travel available, the least painful is the two-engined airplane which requires just forty-five minutes for the trip. One alternative is a jouncing, mud- or dust-coated journey by automobile; the other a jouncing, soot-coated journey by train. The former alternative is quicker and is made over roads designated on the map as "Class A," which means that, if the driver can only nego-

tiate the impassable sections of the road, it is passable throughout the wet and the less-wet seasons of the year. The trip by
rail is slower, but it does provide the elegance of a porter,
who periodically during the eight- to ten-hour trip passes
through the first-class compartments with a brush to desoot
the passengers—with but temporary success. None of these
journeys is dangerous, but those by land rather than by air
are monotonous, for the Ghana landscape presents little of
interest.

This part of Africa consists largely of low-lying, gently
rolling hills, at an elevation of about eight hundred feet. The
prospect would be pleasant enough if it could be seen, but
once the narrow coastal plain has been traversed, the tropical
rain forest spraddles its huge trees and dense undergrowth
directly in the line of vision in all directions, making this the
greenest of green worlds.

Across the Pra River, traditional but often breached barri-
cade between the Ashanti and their less widely organized
Akan relatives to the south, lies the land of the proud people.
An Ashanti lives with his nearly 850,000 proud fellow men
in the central portion of Ghana, where for two centuries his
ancestors had been developing a way of life so complex as
to make it unusual in comparison with the rest of the nonliterate world which is ordinarily more simply organized. It
may have been no more or less satisfying than the more
simple cultures, no more or less satisfying than the still more
complex cultures of the literate world, but it was the creation of his ancestors and it is his creation. He is proud of it,
and its intricate and satisfying features demand understanding lest it be regarded as just another backward part of the
world.

26

"Ashanti," sometimes misleadingly identified in crossword puzzles as "a warlike tribe of West Africa," refers both to the territory and to the people who inhabit it. Some two hundred fifty years ago a small cluster of related, small states began to organize a confederacy, some being incorporated by conquest, others by voluntary agreement—though not without some pressure. By the late nineteenth century there had developed a government of imperial cast and of remarkable political complexity for the nonliterate world, being bureaucratic and hierarchic in its structure but using a principle of decentralization of authority which permitted the member states to manage all affairs which did not affect the Confederacy.

At the summit of the Confederacy stood the king, the Asantehene. Actually "sat" is a better word, for the Golden Stool, miraculously created and delivered by the gods and ancestors, was the emblem of his authority, the evidence of his unique, sacred ordination. At his side stood the Asanteman Council, composed of the paramount chiefs of the member states of the Confederacy, near equals to the Asantehene in the direction of Ashanti affairs. They, with their designated subordinates, each represented their states in the central government while simultaneously holding a position of chiefly power, parallel to that of the Asantehene, in their own states. As paramount chiefs of their states, they governed with a council comprised of the appropriate representatives of districts within their states, and district chiefs similarly served their smaller areas with a council composed of town or village chiefs. Within these communities the town chief or village head served as a leader in steady consultation with a council made up of the heads of the families resident in the community. On each level of the hierarchy the chief was picked only from among the members of the one traditionally desig-

27

nated royal family, but choice from this number of eligible persons required the approval of the constituent commoner groups, and a poor selection could be deposed by popular demand. Even this simplified table of organization reveals a logic and a degree of democratization that was capable of providing stable government with the consent of the governed.

The armies of the Ashanti Confederacy threatened both the smaller African states and the Europeans all the way south to the Atlantic Ocean, and undoubtedly only the presence of the British military, with its African mercenaries and colonial subjects, prevented the Confederacy from becoming an even more powerful West African empire. Finally, after several unsuccessful expeditions—halfhearted, to be sure—the British captured Kumasi, the capital of Ashanti, in 1898, deposed and deported the Asantehene, crushed a subsequent rebellion, and in 1901 declared the land to be a colony of the crown. Even in defeat the Ashanti never completely lost their dignity, and the affirmation "the British never defeated us" can still be heard in the land, although the land may not thoroughly agree with the boast.

Ashanti's people live in a territory of 24.4 thousand square miles, an area about one-half the size of the state of New York. Kumasi is the capital and is its one major city. Its approximately 85,000 inhabitants and those who dwell in the lesser cities of the state make up only about 20 per cent of the population.

Kumasi is rich in the proud history and traditions of the people; it was—and is—the heart of the Ashanti Confederacy. It is here that the king, the Asantehene, resides, and it is here that the Golden Stool, the compelling symbol of Ashanti power, glory, and unity, is kept in sacred state. The city and

its symbolic significance for the Ashanti people are under-
going changes akin to those occurring throughout all the areas
of the world in which Europeans have exerted their revolutionary influence for a generation or more. But the city and
the position it holds in the Ashanti world view still reflect the
aura of what until sixty years ago was a growing African empire. It commands the respect of nearly one million Ashanti
and the attention—sometimes disrespectful, but nonetheless
attention—of more than three million other citizens of Ghana.

It is here that the Golden Stool, symbol of ancestral and
divine authority for the Ashanti Confederacy, was first revealed; it is near here that the first links of the Confederacy
were forged more than two and a half centuries ago; it is here
that the armies were marshaled to extend the bounds of the
nation and the politicians and diplomats sealed the treaties
which incorporated into the nation those states sensible
enough to yield peaceably. To Kumasi came the chiefs of the
member states to represent their people in the councils of
the Confederacy and to wield the authority shrewdly dele-
gated to each in the interest of unity and power. Sixty years of
British domination have not completely eradicated the sense
of divine sanction and temporal authority which spurred the
Confederacy to its successes and which has persisted, if
tarnished, through its defeats. Kumasi may have the sociologi-
cal appearance of a small city which functions as a center
for commerce, government, and politics, for transport and
education, for secondary services, and for loafers, hoodlums,
and agitators. Its politicians may approach their problems
with a greater degree of cold rationality; they may even con-
sciously manipulate the ancient symbols with a calloused ap-
preciation of their propaganda value. But the sacred traditions
of the Ashanti which find their most dramatic expression in

the city of Kumasi, in its people and their institutions, cannot yet be ignored.

Kumasi is the real Ashanti. But most of the people are in the country, and they, too, are the real Ashanti. The Ashanti are a predominantly rural people; fully 80 per cent of the population lives in small towns, villages, and hamlets. At most the population density averages about 35 per square mile, and in the Ahafo District in western Ashanti, the home of the people of this book, the density is only 16. Goaso is a farmers' town of 1,000 people in the Ahafo District. For those who wish to go there, another Class A road winds westward from Kumasi. Over its pockmarked, washboard surface trucks and automobiles jolt and grind through numerous towns and villages along the 85-mile route. Now and then the hulk of some monstrous tree spans the road where it has collapsed with a thunderous death roar. Dissected by hand ax and motor saw, it is pulled aside by the very people who once would have allowed it to lie in peace. Now they are going places—to Goaso, to Kumasi, to Accra, to London, to Burma, perhaps to fight in a world war, to New York, to Urbana, Illinois, and other American college towns, and their path crosses the very spot where the old African giant has fallen.

Little more than fifty years ago few people bothered actually to come to Goaso, but today this town's streets and lanes carry the soft, dignified tread of the proud, sandaled feet of village and district chiefs, sometimes even of Kumasi chiefs. When the British Empire first marched in, Goaso's few households huddled near the riverbank. The town's appearance and position have altered favorably during the ensuing years, for Goaso was selected as the site of the British administrator for the Ahafo District of the Ashanti Colony. Almost continually since that time assistant district commissioners—more recently called government agents, in keeping with the changing political fortunes—have been in residence in the rambling, cool house on the hill, and a steady parade of chiefs and lesser figures has helped to elevate the town and its 1,000 inhabitants to a rank where they now merit recognition on the *National Geographic* map of Africa.

The government agent is not pictured in this book, but his well-accepted presence and the presence of that which he represents can be felt throughout its pages. The coming of the British, with their administrators and governmental bureaucrats, high and low and in-between, with their trading companies for buying cocoa and selling cloth, kerosene, Pepsodent, gin, and many other useful things, with their roads and trucks, with their missionaries and schoolteachers, their medical science and college educations, has worked rash changes in the Goaso way of life. Only a handful of Europeans have lived in the Ahafo District—only one, the agent, in Goaso—but their shadows are to be seen everywhere; in the desires of the Africans for numerous European goods and services and for profits; in economic institutions such as the trading stores, co-operatives, and warehouses in which the lucrative cash crop, cocoa, is stored prior to its shipment to the chocolate-hungry Europeans and Americans—especially the Americans; in the religious institutions, such as the Methodist and the Roman Catholic churches; in the schools, with their overflowing classrooms and harried teachers.

Where the road enters Goaso a modern cement bridge spans the Goa River, but a path along the stream's bank leads to the quiet, vine-tangled pool near the place which for many decades has supplied the water for drinking, cooking, and bathing, and for the unwanted breeding of malarial mosquitoes. The women and children of many generations have walked gracefully through the damp dawn to the river to draw the water for their households' daily needs, and the first duty of the day remains unchanged. The bridge is new, the kerosene cans in which the water is carried are new, the gasoline drums in which the water is stored are new, and the preventive and curative drugs which fight malaria are new, but the river is old, and the people of Goaso, "on the banks of the Goa River," have long depended upon the stream for the life both of the body and of the spirit. The Goa is one of innumerable streams which drain the area of its heavy rains, provide the water of life, and shelter the holy places where gods have revealed themselves to their people.

Few Europeans ever stop for long in Goaso. As recently as 1951 only the bachelor government agent had a permanent residence there. For˙reasons probably appreciated only by themselves, an American anthropologist and his wife reached the agreeable decision to stay there for a visit of eight months several years ago and were cordially, if quizzically, welcomed. A lone Dutch Roman Catholic priest trekked in and out of the forest every six weeks or so, sometimes carrying with him a fever of over 100 degrees; if he stayed through Sunday he celebrated a Mass; if not, he reviewed—usually with some dismay—the operation and finances of the Roman Catholic school. Two or three times a year a Methodist missionary found cause to visit the local church. Infrequent appearances were also put in by the European or African personnel of the Department of Education, Posts and Telegraphs, the cocoa co-operative, or some other branch of government. Half a dozen British lumber mill operators did their best to make a profit and to remember England in a town eight miles away, but they found little in Goaso to attract them; ordinarily they ground through town in their jeeps or trucks, begrimed by the red dirt of 85 miles of gritty Class A road, hauling mahogany for somebody's dining-room table in Chelsea. But if these Europeans and those who stood behind them were only occasionally seen, they were and are strongly felt. Except for them, these pages would not read as they do.

Goaso and the Ahafo District lie within the tropical rain forest region. Water drips or streams from the skies throughout most of the year, to an annual fall of between 80 and 100 inches. On only a few occasions does the rain fall for more than a few hours, and even during the wettest weeks of the rainy seasons, in April and July, the sun is not completely vanquished. Frequently toward midafternoon the black clouds scud low and the forest trembles and moans under the rush of the approaching rain-express. The storm rolls through, pouring its water on the warm earth for perhaps an hour, then rumbles on, to return the next afternoon. From December to February the rains avoid this region, the streams grow thin, the earth parched under the steadfast sun, the cisterns low, the dust high. But then, on a late February afternoon, the forest sighs again, the muffled roar grows louder, and another yearly cycle is begun. Temperatures during the year seldom reach as low as 60 degrees or as high as 100 degrees, although during the dry season, when the dry, harmattan wind blows in from the north, the cool air is shivery and the warm air beastly.

The lush forest growth surrounding Goaso creates an impression of Edenic fertility which the soil analysts have discovered is not actually present. In common with most tropical areas of the world, Goaso's land has suffered from leaching, a process in which the topsoil grows progressively thinner in depth and richness as the action of sun and rain over long spans of time destroy and carry away the potassium, phosphate, and other nutrient salts necessary for the production of the better food plants. Behind her smiling mask of greenery, Mother Nature has frowned on vast areas of the tropics. Despite her—in Goaso the people would claim "with her"—the Africans, without artificial fertilizers, have devised a system of shifting cultivation which has enabled the population to produce its basic food supply and, during the past forty or fifty years, to add the cultivation of a cash crop, cocoa, to their agricultural production. Cocoa is a semipermanent crop, the trees bearing their lucrative fruit for nearly thirty years, but foodstuffs can be grown on the land for a period of only a few years. When the yield diminishes beyond a certain point, the farm is abandoned and allowed to lie fallow for many years, while successive new plots of ground are cleared from the forest, harvested of their bounty, then returned to rest and to await the axes and hoes of the next generation.

This method of shifting cultivation has proved satisfactory enough to the Africans to make them primarily dependent upon agriculture—or, better, gardening—for their food supply. Thus the land itself and its natural and cultivated fruits have come to assume a place of great moment in the possessions and aspirations of Goaso and all Ashanti, an importance which, it will be seen, is reflected in their religious, political, and other social ideals.

In this setting, then, lies Goaso. Its single-storied, block-like, unspectacular, though dignified even when crumbling, baked mud homes rest between the road to Kumasi on one side and the soccer-football field on the other. The football field is now a familiar though not quite integral part of nearly

every Ashanti village. On Sunday afternoons the countryside
is alive with perspiring young amateurs building stalwart
character and acquiring with each solid kick those qualities
of gentlemanly competitiveness and sportsmanship and of
co-operative teamwork which, as every citizen of the English-
speaking world knows, are the natural outcome of competitive
sports, be the fields at Eton, South Bend, or Goaso. The path
cutting across the field leads to the home of the British administrative agent, who frequently comes down the path to
serve as referee when Goaso entertains the teams from
Hwidiem or Nobekaw or other towns farther down the road.
Most of the townspeople enjoy the game from the sidelines,
cheering on their nimble, barefoot heroes while the somewhat
less agile, largely self-taught musicians in the band rhyth-
mically sweat and blow their way through traditional African
tunes played in modern styles on British brass instruments
imperfectly mastered.

It's fun, and there is always the possibility of winning a bet
from one of the visiting partisans. Perhaps he doesn't realize
that beneath the uprights defended by Goaso there lies buried
a magical charm which in past games has proved itself capable
of deflecting even the most accurate placement by the enemy.
Before actually putting up the money, however, the local
bettor had better make certain that the ground beneath the
Goaso goal hasn't recently been disturbed. Visiting teams
have been known to go to the most absurd lengths to win a
game, even to the extent of employing magic. Regardless of
which team wins, the band concludes the afternoon of sport
with a dance procession through the town. Tunes like "Evah-
body love Sataday Night" and "The Jaguah Cah" are "tooooo
good." In dancing, everybody wins.

If the football field brings a touch of England to Goaso,

the town itself presents an appearance more traditionally Ashanti. One main street bisects the town and intersects the main road which snakes on past Goaso to Mim and other road-hungry towns farther north and south. A solitary tree, half denuded of its foliage by raucous birds, shades the checker players and loafers and defends the street against a motorized civilization. Both principal residential sections of town are crisscrossed by narrower parallel lanes which separate the evenly spaced homes from each other. Across the road, on lower, less desirable ground, is the Zongo quarter, allocated to the Moslem "strangers" or aliens who reside here as trades-men cr farm laborers. The rooms fronting on the road and the street generally serve as the shops and workrooms of crafts-men and storekeepers, and their overhanging roofs shelter the salesmen and their wares.

Back from the road are the homes, more than seventy of them, housing most of Goaso's 1,000 people. Designed simply in rectangular form, the four sides, each one room in depth, enclose a large central courtyard entered by a single narrow passageway. Within these walls, and especially within the courtyard during the day, the members of the household find their living space for cooking and eating, for sleeping and visit-ing, for planning and plotting, for working and playing, for rearing children and caring for the sick and the aged, for nearly everything essential to living well and eventually to dying well. Members of the household occupy a series of adjacent rooms, eight to twelve in number, located around four sides of the central courtyard. One of these rooms, usually lacking its inner wall, provides storage and cooking space, while the others serve as sleeping and sitting rooms for the ten to twenty persons who dwell there.

Although a few of the newer buildings are being constructed

36

of durable cement blocks, most of Goaso's residences are designed and built according to long-familiar, traditional patterns. One of two construction methods is usually adopted. In the first, low walls of clay, dug from a nearby site, are built according to the design of the completed residence. After the clay has dried thoroughly, a second segment is added on top, and, when this has dried, the third and fourth segments are built up until the walls have reached a height of six or more feet. To protect each segment against the rain, a covering of palm branches is placed upon it. Cracks, which have developed during drying, are filled in, and all surfaces, interior and exterior, smoothed over. Next, the roof is put in place. Formerly of thatch, it is now constructed of corrugated tin in the British-inspired interests of decreasing the hazards of fire, disease-laden rodents, and one hundred and one species of small animal life distasteful to Europeans and hardly beneficial to the Africans who tolerated them. The tin roof makes for a more costly and hotter but, all in all, healthier room, and the eight- to twelve-inch thickness of the clay walls helps to keep down the heat.

Room temperatures are also affected by the use of windows. Almost invariably viewed with suspicion, the windows are generally kept shuttered and locked, thus effectively preventing the entrance of both air and thieves. The result is a series of fairly cool, dark rooms, used for little but sleeping and for storing personal valuables, all of them opening only onto the central courtyard where most of life is lived under the sun and the stars.

In the second principal type of house construction, vertical and horizontal poles are lashed together, and mud is slapped into place. Finishing is performed in the same manner as in the method described above. Either method provides a livable

37

residence for a period of about thirty years, after which the walls gradually weary of their work and slump to the ground. When the traffic in the remaining rooms gets too heavy, a new home is built nearby.

Having already outlived its allotted one score and ten years, Goaso faces an extensive rebuilding problem, and many families have already moved into new homes about a half mile up the road. The more affluent members of society have hired migrant laborers to perform much of the work, carpenters and roofers to build the roof, and contractors to organize and oversee the construction. The less well-to-do still follow the traditional pattern of do-it-yourself with the co-operation of members of the large family and of friends, all of whom join in, motivated by the prospect of a good time, of plenty of food and drink provided by the owners, and of the future reciprocal aid of those for whom they have worked. Any family contemplating a new home must now figure on expenditures of nearly $1,000, and costs of more elaborate dwellings may run to five or six times that amount.

Not content with completely traditional styles, the more successful families in Ashanti symbolize their superiority by adding embellishments to their homes. An overhanging roof supported by columns, the facing of the walls with cement and the application of white paint with black trim, the installation of panes of glass protected by iron grillwork rather than boards or shutters in the windows, an indoor toilet, all give a mark of distinction to those able to afford such luxuries.

The interior courtyard of the better homes is paved with cement blocks, but the ordinary homes here use only the good earth, trodden down by years and at least three generations of bare or sandaled feet. The courtyard, seldom deserted, carries the real burden and joy of living, for it is here that the housekeeping is performed, the meals prepared, the washing hung out to dry, the cloth dyed, the children tended. It is here that womanly gossip is originated and exchanged, that manly plans are laid; here the young girls learn their womanly skills and the boys their manly arts; here the goats and chickens rum· mage for tasty scraps; here the cocoa bean, which will eventually pay for the next courtyard, is placed to dry in the sun. In the courtyard the visitor is received, the greetings exchanged, the liquid refreshments proffered and accepted, the news reported.

There is important news these days, too; news from Hwidiem, just down the road, where a new school is being built; from Kumasi, much farther down the road, where the chiefs and politicians are arguing over the future role of Ashanti in national Ghana politics; from Accra, down by the sea, where the Legislative Council and the prime minister, elected in part by Goaso's votes, are arguing about the position the traditional chiefs should have in the democratic parliamentary system of a modern state and about Ashanti's secessionist moods. There is news, too, from London, where the Queen and her government and the banks and firms revise old relationships with the new member of the British Commonwealth—and there are millions of people, dark-skinned and light-skinned, to satisfy. The courtyard hums.

Few homes are so ill equipped as to lack a private washroom where all may take, modestly, their daily baths. Occasionally, very occasionally, a tiled shower room and the flashing chrome of modern plumbing fixtures reveal a high peak of worldly success and modernity. Not many homes, however, are equipped for the disposal of human wastes; for this, the public latrines just beyond the edge of town serve the youth and adults; the lanes serve the very young.

39

At least one room in many homes—though not in all—holds a special significance which really makes a series of rooms into a home. Although at most times it may be treated as just one more room, on certain occasions it becomes a shrine, to be approached with solemnity and great dignity, with shoulder bared and feet unshod in awe and respect for its sacred nature. For this is the room in which are kept the remembrances and symbols of the ancestors who for many generations have built their homes in this place, have worked their lands, have preserved the proud traditions of each family, and have made a good life possible for this generation. In style this room resembles any other; it may function as a sleeping room and storeroom. But that which distinguishes it from all others is the row of gracefully carved, smoke-blackened, low, wooden seats or stools—there may be just one—of those men or women who have been the leaders of this family in the past. On those occasions when their glory is being remembered and their presence acknowledged, this room becomes a temple. If a home has no such room, it is not that the family is without its own glory, but only that it remembers and reveres the ancestors whose symbols are kept in the central home of the larger family of which it is a branch.

For a home is not a home, a family is not a family, individuals are not individuals unless all have the perspective of themselves as merely the current mortal representatives of the ageless line of ancestors, those creators and guardians of the present. Here and there may be found a house which has neither shrine nor remembrance. If it is because of misfortune or migration, this house is deeply to be pitied; if it is because of modernism, it is regrettable that such things happen. There are not yet many such empty homes—the one home with the tile shower room and the chrome fixtures has a room for the ancestors. But the number of ancestorless houses is slowly increasing.

When the rituals of respect to the past have been performed, the home furnishings of the present once more come into view. Ghana is a land rich in mahogany, and the Westerner sighs with disbelief and envy as his heavy shoes clump across flooring of this treasured wood. Furniture, too, is of mahogany, and most rooms are equipped with a chest of drawers, a table, and a simply designed, heavy, unupholstered chair or two. Mirrors on the walls reflect a distorted but still recognizable image of the proud owner, and a brass bedstead occupies an inordinately large part of the 10' x 10' room. The pleasure of sleeping in a brass bedstead has been extolled by the market-hungry British manufacturers of brass bedsteads, and the luxury of life with mahogany chests of drawers, tables, and chairs has been extolled by the market-hungry African carpenters who exploit the growing demands for standardized European styles of furniture. Willing to be persuaded and able to pay, the Africans are buying.

One other piece of furniture in many rooms reflects the intermingling of the sacred world with the secular; it is the wooden box in which are kept the most prized, though not necessarily the most costly, possessions of the owner: some gold dust or coins or pound notes, some cloth, some papers or permits, some charms to help ensure health, prosperity, and success, and other intimate items which are regarded as integral parts of the person himself. Such things, frequently inconsequential in themselves, are greatly beloved and in some way identified with their owner's soul. They are elements of the individual's inviolable self, his personal holy of holies. At times of frustration or depression or anger they

41

may be removed and a ritual privately performed in order to purge the soul of its anxiety and restore it to health.

Other rooms are variously furnished; sitting rooms may be equipped with a table and chairs, tablecloths, pictures on the wall—the Asantehene and the Queen of England, placed side by side, are favorites—rugs of woven grasses, porcelain knickknacks, and odds and ends. Some sleeping rooms are furnished only with sleeping mats upon the hard floor. In any case, the nearly ubiquitous mosquito netting hangs suspended from ceiling to couch to screen out all except the tiniest of the insect hordes.

The kitchen, a room left open on its interior side, is simply equipped with an open hearth of low clay mounds, a few iron pots for cooking, some containers of pottery or basketry, a heap of firewood, a wooden mortar and pestle used in the grinding of favorite foods, supplies for the evening meal, and quite possibly, the few remains of recent meals.

These are simple things for the most part, a rectangular dwelling, unspectacular rooms, chairs, iron pots, candles and kerosene lamps, and the other relatively uncomplicated material things which are necessary for living in Goaso. But there is more to living than these paltry goods. There are the ancestors and the gods, all of whom are necessary to the success of even the most humble venture. When a site is cleared for a new home, the family and friends and the chief of the town gather to ask a benediction upon the land and upon the occupants. The ancestors and gods are called to attend, and the hospitality of this generation is offered through the spilling of liquor and the dropping of morsels of food upon the ground. Again when the new home is completed, a similar invocation is spoken and the gods and ancestors are invited to come bringing prosperity and peace and long life and all highest satisfactions to the household. So that the ancestors may rest when, unseen, they visit their descendants, their stools are placed in an honored and respected place. There they are kept, too, so that the growing child may always know that he is not alone in the world, but that he is in the effective company of the ancestral hosts.

While the friends and more remote relatives remain outside the new home, the heart of the family—those brothers who have built the home, their mother and her brothers, their sisters, and their father—gathers with the chief of the town in the courtyard of the new home now to be dedicated. Here, with trembling hands and voice, bespeaking the awe and emotion of a mortal who stands in the presence of the gods and ancestors who have made this happy event possible, the chief pours a few drops of gin or palm wine upon the ground while asking the benediction of the spiritual world. The sacramental gin, Gordon's or Gilbey's, flows from a recently imported British bottle, but that is incidental to the reality of the gods and ancestors. They have long been here in Goaso, and they are here today.

4. Meet My Families

Certain social problems which cause great concern in the Western world and which have been solved with only partial success are of relatively little importance in Ashanti. There are no orphanages, no homes for the aged, no cheap boardinghouses where homeless widows or widowers eke out a colorless existence on tiny pensions hardly large enough to pay last month's bills. There are none, because there is little need for them. It is not that people do not grow old or that parents do not die. Ashanti will never be confused with Eden, and these problems do arise, but the society is organized to solve them with a minimum of personal disruption.

To accomplish this, the Ashanti have worked out a tight network of family and social obligations which make social security, insurance, and annuities unnecessary. Dependence in a crisis is not upon bank accounts. A man does not carry his wealth in his wallet. Instead, the security of the dependent person rests in the respectful hands of other persons, particularly his relatives, to whom he has been and will be throughout his life bound by ties of kinship and of reciprocal rights and obligations to service and co-operation. The person who has no family faces difficulties as great as those faced by the elderly widows of the Western world, but such persons are few in number in Ashanti. The orphans, the aged, the sick,

44

the widowed go home to their families. It is as simple, as effective, as reassuring as that. They go home.

To the Ashanti living in Goaso, "home and family" do not mean precisely the same thing those terms connote to the European or American. To the latter, these comforting words refer for the most part to a few people, a wife or husband, a few children, perhaps a grandparent or two. Some families may even extend out far enough to include some aunts, uncles, and cousins, but a home shared by aunts, uncles, and cousins is not the happiest home, even if they are only staying overnight. Not so in Goaso; here "home and family" means plenty of relatives, living and working and playing and worrying as a well-knit unit in a single or neighboring household. This un-Western aspect of "the family" requires a little explanation.

To begin, "the family" is not a small, single unit. It is a unified group, to be sure, but the total group consists of a number of integrated parts, each of which functions in its own sphere. The smallest unit, which can be called "the immediate family," is made up of a man, his wife, and their children. Within this group, the husband and father is responsible for providing the others with their food, their shelter and clothing, for everything essential to a satisfactory life. As the children grow older, their father's responsibilities to them decrease, but during their childhood he is the person upon whom they depend.

Usually the members of this immediate family live together, although many men prefer to live separately from them in another household in town or even in another town. Living elsewhere does not relieve him of his obligations to care for them, for marriage is much more than a convenient, temporary affair, and the husband and father who ignores his duties is liable to find himself the defendant in a suit for divorce, which will prove embarrassing and costly.

Living apart is frequently the arrangement adopted, though not always so, when a man has more than one wife, for the problems of maintaining a home are multiplied when a man is a member of more than one immediate family. Not all men are diplomatic enough to care for several wives and their respective children in a single household—a lack of talent which in any society occasions no surprise. What more discreet solution to a delicate problem could there be than to keep separate establishments for them? At the same time, the versatility, generosity, and impartiality of the husband who can manage a single home for his several immediate families is greatly to be admired. There is in Ashanti, for example, a remarkably able husband who one Christmas delivered six phonographs and six identical sets of records, one to each of his six wives and immediate families. There is an Ashanti worthy of the name. Most men—upward of 75 per cent of them—have only one wife, however, and need not face up to the many-faceted, though by no means insuperable, problems of a polygynous household.

The immediate family is created by a marriage, and a man acquires enough obligations by his marriage to realize that he has got himself into something. But in another important sense the man is not even a member of this group, for, in reality, the immediate family formed by a marriage is made up of two families, each of which is distinct from the other. These two families within the immediate family consist of a husband-and-father, on the one hand, a wife-and-mother and their children, on the other.

The reason for this division is to be found in the Ashanti principle of reckoning family membership by the "matrilineal descent principle." According to this principle, a child belongs only to the family of his mother. His descent is counted only through females; his family is that of his mother, his mother's mother, his mother's mother's mother, back until the roots of his genealogical tree have been reached.

If this system of determining family membership seems a little odd to people raised in a bilineal system—in which a child considers himself equally a member of the families of both his mother and his father—it should be said that it is a perfectly sound system and a very popular one in the non-Western world. Societies using this system, or using the patrilineal system of belonging only to the father's and not to the mother's family, get all the work done necessary to the life of the society.

Nobody knows just how these systems got started; they originated too long ago. But the rather cynical explanation offered by some Ashanti—"you always know who the mother is; you can't always be sure who the father is"—probably doesn't hold water. Certainly it doesn't help explain why, in patrilineal societies, the child belongs only to his father's family. In such a society supposedly "you always know who the father is." The most egotistical male would have difficulty persuading himself of that. Nor is there the slightest evidence to suggest that the Ashanti system represents an early stage in human family life, long ago abandoned by the "advanced, civilized" people of Europe in favor of a bilineal system but still retained by backward peoples. This kind of evolutionary explanation of differences between systems has itself been abandoned by nearly all social scientists. Actually, the matrilineal system is a style, one particular mode acquired historically from among a number of possibilities, learned and maintained by each succeeding generation, and particularly well suited to other features of the society. It has worked satisfactorily for the Ashanti just as the bilineal system has worked satisfactorily in Europe and America. In Ashanti most people simply explain their particular system by pointing out that the ancestors reckoned descent that way. And that, of course, is a basic reason why any society uses the system it does.

Because a person at one and the same time belongs to a family-by-marriage and to a family-by-birth, and because he distinguishes sharply between the two, another family term is necessary. The family-by-birth can be called the "extended family." It is composed of all those people who have descended from a common ancestor several generations ago. Because the Ashanti are matrilineal, that single ancestor is a woman, and all members of the extended family are able to trace their ancestry back through the mothers of each preceding generation to that common ancestress. After four generations or so of this reckoning, the extended family gets pretty large and its branches tend to have less and less to do with each other. At this point a kind of loose boundary line is drawn between two or more extended families: those family members who live in one village are likely to consider themselves as one extended family, while those who have moved elsewhere regard themselves as a separate though related extended family.

Not all ties between separated extended families are completely severed. After all, each of the extended families did descend from a common ancestress and, in recognition of the bonds between them, each family regards itself as a member of a larger kin group called a "lineage." When the common ancestry is traced even further back, a very large number of people, usually living in widely scattered areas but realizing their relationship, consider each other as belonging to the same "clan." There are just eight of these in Ashanti. Members of the same clan, not to mention the same lineage, are thought to be closely enough related to each other as to make marriage or sexual relations between them incestuous, and both, therefore, are forbidden.

Each person, then, belongs to an ever-widening circle of kinship groups-by-birth, and, because marriage to any member of any one of these kin groups is forbidden, his several families-by-birth are kept distinct from his family-by-marriage. A husband, for example, does not belong to the extended family of his wife; she belongs to the family of her mother. She does not become a member of his extended family when they marry, nor does he join her family. A father does not even belong to the family of his children; they belong to the family of their mother, which is the family of her mother and of her mother's mother. A man does belong to the family of his mother and of his mother's mother. Included in his extended family are all those descendants, male or female, of their recognized common ancestress. Those members of his extended family who live either with him or very close to him, and who together form a closely knit group, are his brothers and sisters, his married sisters' children (but not his married brothers' children, for they belong to their mother's family), his mother, his mother's brothers and sisters, and his mother's sister's children.

Extending this logical system back one or two more generations would require some monotonous, tongue-twisting terminology, so a single example will do. Consider that "close relative" in the Ashanti extended family who stands in the relationship of mother's mother's mother's sister's daughter's daughter's daughter. This "relative" in America would be a cousin so far removed as to be treated merely as an acquaintance, if known at all; marriage to her would fail to raise even the most fastidious eyebrow. But this girl, in Ashanti, is an intimate member of the extended family and is treated much as a sister; the thought of marriage to her would shock all except those whose morals have been corrupted by modernism. The inclusion of such biologically distant relatives in the family group gives each individual a large number of persons to depend upon; all of them are required to take a close and, if necessary, sacrificial family interest in his welfare. There are few lonely people in Ashanti.

The importance of the immediate family, which is really made up of two distinct extended families, lineages, and clans, should not be minimized, for both mutual affection and obligations accepted in the marriage agreement draw and keep a husband-and-father together with his wife and children throughout most if not all of life. These obligations extend beyond the married couple as well, for a marriage is between extended families as well as between individuals. The two families so joined come to rely upon each other and to affirm their pledged unity on numerous occasions. As the years pass, however, children born to a family-by-marriage gradually loosen the ties with their father; with the approach of puberty, and later of young manhood and finally of adulthood, the relationships between a child and his father come more and more to rest upon simple affection and mutual respect and less and less upon formal obligation. A daughter is drawn more and more exclusively into the family of her birth, that is, her mother's family. A son comes more and more to substitute his mother's brother for his father as the most important man in his life, because, of course, a young man's mother's brother is a member of his own family, while his father is not. Simultaneously, the father acquires more and more obligations to his sister's sons, who, in turn, look increasingly to him as their guardian and benefactor. The ties between father and children are never severed, but they are gradually relaxed as the generations grow older.

Leadership in an extended family or lineage usually falls to an older, male member of the family because of the superior wisdom and experience he has acquired during his lifetime. Subject always to the approval of the other members of the extended family, he carries the greatest weight in making economic or other social decisions affecting the family. In the control of wealth in land, in farms and buildings, or other large concentrations of value, great, though not absolute, authority rests with the head-of-the-family. At his death, his authority is almost automatically bequeathed to the next in age of his brothers—unless that person is generally regarded as physically, intellectually, or morally unfit for the position—until, at last, death has carried all the members of that elder generation to the ancestral world, from which they continue to exert their invisible leadership. It is at this time that the gradually strengthened relationship between the mother's brothers and their nephews becomes especially important, for, with the death of the uncles, the sister's sons become eligible for leadership in the extended family.

During the years of his approaching manhood the nephew has benefited from the wealth controlled by his uncle, and he has been well taught to care for and increase it. Now that the last of the uncles has died, he is fully prepared to take his uncle's place and to look forward to the time when his own sister's sons will come to him for their training in the arts of leadership. Then, if all goes well, he will journey finally to the land of his ancestors, there to join them in the rewarding observation of the skills he helped to develop in his sister's sons. The father of the sons, meanwhile, is not concerned with their inheritance of wealth and leadership; his responsibilities lie within his own extended family and lineage, in the education of his own nephews to the point where they can carry the traditions of his family with honor and distinction.

Certain strains in this fabric of matrilineal family relationships have begun to appear in recent years. From one side there comes the push of European and Christian social and religious beliefs which emphasize the overriding obligations of a father to his own children throughout their lifetimes. Persistently the literature and teachings of the Europeans encourage the Ashanti to maximize their attentions upon the immediate family—that family composed of husband, wife, and children—and to minimize their interests in the extended family and the lineage, to care for their sons and daughters rather than for their nieces and nephews. This family and religious emphasis is "natural" for Europeans who, after all, were not taught when they pray to say, "Our mother's brother, who art in heaven . . ." The dominant branches of the Christian church have developed in more or less patrilineal, patriarchal societies, and they have, quite naturally, encouraged the father-son relationship to the exclusion of the matrilineal uncle-nephew relationship.

From the other side there comes the pull of changing economic conditions which make more difficult the fulfillment of traditional obligations. Ashanti fatherhood has never been characterized by an absence of obligations. During all of their preadolescent period and, to a lessening degree, during young manhood a father is responsible for the rearing of his children; only if he proves derelict in his duties does the children's uncle assume early responsibility for them. Most fathers, like most fathers anywhere, are good fathers and seek to discharge their duties as fathers should. But to do so in modern times requires a greater investment in energy and expense than previously. Education, formerly a normal function of the immediate and extended families, now requires school attendance, the payment of tuition and fees, the expense of uniforms and books, the burden of increased taxes, and the constant drain of sixpences and shillings which school children collect constantly. A boy and girl in the schoolroom, furthermore, are a boy and girl fewer in the field, and their labor must be replaced, usually at additional expense and frequently over a period of from six to ten or more years.

In addition, the amounts of wealth have increased in Goaso and elsewhere in Ashanti because of the success of cocoa growing as a lucrative agricultural enterprise. Sons, who invest much of their time during childhood and youth on their father's cocoa farms, resentfully watch the rich fruits of their labors slipping away to their father's sisters' children. Meanwhile, their own future security rests in part upon the increasingly uncertain efforts of their mother's brothers' sons, boys whose faithfulness to traditional obligations may be undermined by the substitute attractions of modernity. Fathers, uncles, sons, nephews are leaving home more frequently to work elsewhere, and the families are becoming dispersed; when families become separated by many miles, by newly acquired interests, and by differing degrees of economic success, the traditional moral obligations are more easily and frequently ignored. Grave anxieties as to the predictability of future behavior arise, and the family control of its members weakens. The old securities are no longer quite so secure. The old days, the old, sure systems are slipping away.

Such dilemmas as these combine to raise questions about the wisdom of the matrilineal descent system in the changed society which is emerging. But in Goaso, until now, these have been no more than questions to be worried over rather than acted upon. The still well-understood, reassuring traditional system is changing but slowly even in the face of what may eventually be recognized as incompatible circumstances.

In any culture, some ideals and patterns of behavior change more slowly than others. Even in the United States, in what is generally considered to be a rational, change-oriented society, traditional and basically individualistic solutions to social security problems were retained until little more than two decades ago, and even now a systematized, government-directed social security program is roundly ridiculed by a minority of individualists. If such changes could be achieved but slowly in a society which was obviously in need of readjustment in these respects, it is hardly surprising that there should be resistance to changing a system of social security which in Ashanti once worked well. But in time the changes, for good or ill, will come.

An Ashanti boy meets an Ashanti girl, and what happens? The preceding discussion of immediate families, extended families, lineages, clans, mother's brothers and sister's sons, matrilineal descent principles, and social security tells something of what happens. But what about the boy and girl? As is customary in Ashanti, they marry. But as usual it isn't quite so simple as that; it seldom is, and certainly it is not simple in Ashanti.

The story of their marriage starts back a few years. In

54

fact, it starts back quite a few generations, for, in the beginning, he and she must have had separate, unrelated ancestresses. The cardinal principle to follow is "never caress the ear of a fellow clan member." Of all the sins against the ancestors, incest, mating with a clansman—foreshadowed by some amorous ear-pulling—is among the most horrifying and dangerous.

The girl is not related to the boy. She is the daughter of his mother's brother—in matrilineal Ashanti, a perfectly marriageable relationship. And she is ready to marry, for the proud announcement of her entrance into womanhood has already been sung to the world. She is ready to marry, and so is he.

She became marriageable when she reached puberty. With the onset of her first menstruation her proud family began preparations for her maidenly debut into adult society, for her assumption of those roles most important to the living of a full and happy life—the bearing and rearing of children. Then, during a glorious, weeklong celebration, her girlishness was tenderly bathed away, and she emerged a mature woman among women. For seven magnificent days she was required only to bask in the delight of being an Ashanti woman. During those splendid days her relatives and friends besieged her with their lavish gifts; pendants and chains of finely wrought gold were hung about her neck and arms; intricately woven garments of golden and brilliant hues were draped about her delightfully formed young body, leaving her breasts bared as a symbol of her maturity and of the motherhood she hoped soon to enjoy. Each day the elderly women of her family carried her to the river, where all impurities and the vestiges of childhood were washed away; her soft skin was groomed with oil until she glistened in beauty and honor. Gold dust was sprinkled in abandon over her graceful shoulders and arms, and a few lines of bright pigments illumined the striking features of her youthful face. Attended by an envying court of younger girls, she walked with maidenly shyness and innocent pride about the lanes of the village, visiting the homes of all who knew her. Her attendants shrilled girlish songs, happy that she had become a woman and anticipating the pleasures and respected duties which soon would be hers. The older women, too, followed her through the town, singing of their youth and well-remembered but no longer so well-enjoyed pleasures. The words were lusty in keeping with the pleasures, lusty but not vulgar. And she knew, though probably not from experience, what the songs were about.

At the end of the week the girl had become a woman. Within a year or two, at the most, she would marry, and after that she and all her families would await the coming of her first child.

Our Ashanti boy had entered manhood much more quietly. Adulthood for him depended less upon biological maturity than upon the ability to do the economic and social work of men, and he was in his early twenties by the time he was ready to marry. No public celebration honored his arrival; he just came more and more to look like a man, to act like a man, and to be a man.

But they were still not quite ready for marriage, for marriage in Ashanti is not to be taken lightly. Love does have something to do with it, but not much. Sexual relations are regarded by the Ashanti as important, neither sacred nor sinful, but important enough to be carefully regulated. They erect no latticework around sex, open enough to peek through and closed enough to act as a barrier, but they do remind youngsters that premarital experimentation is insulting to the ancestors as well as to the family and to the whole society. Girls and boys approaching their teens are kept pretty well separated in their play, so as to avoid both the temptation and the appearance of wrong, and in the old days a premarital pregnancy was frequently considered so shameful as to be punished by the banishment of the offending couple from the community—a terribly severe penalty when the dependence of an individual upon his kin is remembered. Before the Europeans came, a test for virginity was part of the ritual of the wedding night, and failure to produce the evidence of purity, a stained bedcloth, meant some stabbing ridicule from the townspeople during the next days. Such persuasive threats as these are no longer applied, but the preference for premarital chastity is still maintained.

Unmarried girls who fail to display shyness toward men and boys their age are less desirable than those who do. Girls who attend coeducational secondary schools are thought to be less shy than most. The number of schoolgirls—including Christian mission schoolgirls no less than others—who succumb is, it is rumored, morally staggering to the defenders of the good old days when sexual morality was treasured. The Ashanti have never been puritanical in their attitudes toward sex and the rules have undoubtedly always been broken. But the emphasis has been upon careful control of sexual behavior, and the fear of consequences of discovery has limited the frequency and reduced the presumed pleasure of illicit romance.

This nonpermissive attitude toward premarital promiscuity also carries over into adult, marital behavior, although, as in most societies in which men hold at least a slightly upper hand, the double standard is applied. Extramarital activities are less reprehensible for men than for women, until a point is reached at which a wife feels she is suffering a grievous hardship. Then she may ask her husband's family to restrain him from his philandering or, failing that, she may seek a divorce. But she isn't permitted to do so if her husband is only slightly or occasionally wayward; he must be a frequent offender of her rights and sensibilities. She, on the other hand, had better remain a paragon of sexual virtue, keeping herself only unto him, or she will find herself the defendant in a suit for divorce. At the very least she is liable to be dragged into a public disclosure of her faithlessness in a suit brought against her paramour by her husband, whose argument is, in effect, that the lover has trespassed upon "property" to which he had no rights and must, therefore, pay a fee to the outraged husband for having done so. The lover pays in cash, the wife in shame. And the husband, his insulted soul appeased, vows privately never to conduct his own affairs in so clumsy a fashion as his wife's lover displayed.

The essential seriousness of marriage is reflected not only in these regulations but in the restrictions placed upon the individual in selecting his marriage partner. This is far from unusual in human cultures, for even the most individualistic societies subtly instill marriage prohibitions and prescriptions into their young.

In Ashanti, marriage is less an agreement entered into by two individuals before God or the justice of the peace than it is a social contract between two families, each represented by a partner to the marriage. In America, he and she—subtly conditioned, of course, to know what to look for in a potential mate and thrown together by the conditions of group life— agree to marry; the in-laws approve, attend the parties and the wedding, and then, for the most part, continue to go their separate ways. In Ashanti, potential in-laws first investigate each other and agree to establish new, important obligations of mutual respect and aid between the families; only then may he and she marry. Because a marriage binds two large families closely together it is not to be entered into inadvisedly, but reverently, discreetly, and in fear of the social consequences of an ill-conceived union. The families of both young people are, therefore, active counselors during the courtship, and their wholehearted endorsement is essential to the success of the marriage.

The criteria applied to the two and to their families are, for the most part, familiar. How old is she; has she been married previously; why did her earlier marriage fail; does she possess the personality of a good woman; is she educated in the womanly arts; will she work hard; will she bear many children; will she raise her children well; does she come from a fine family; is the history of her family such as to give pride to anyone allied with it; is it a prosperous family; is her family free from the taints of indebtedness and sorcery; is she from a powerful family; is she from a royal family or, at least, from a free family rather than from a slave family? So the investigation goes, and it is conducted with great care and thoroughness. There need be no embarrassment, for her family is asking the very same questions about his family. And the inquiries are made by the families; no questions of such import, no answers of such consequence, can be entrusted to two youngsters who are just now taking their first hesitant steps in the adult world. This is a job for many old experienced heads, full of the wisdom of the years, not for the young empty heads of a boy and girl who think they like each other.

Ranking first among the questions are those into the possible kinship relationships between the two families. Of what clan is her family? Kin are recognized in ever-widening circles,

and descent from a common ancestress, even in vaguely remembered antiquity, makes of one blood all those so descended; marriage to a member of the same matrilineal clan,
even to one so far removed as a tenth or twentieth "cousin,"
is forbidden as horribly incestuous. Although the restrictions
against marriage to certain relatives on the father's side do not
extend out so far, they must, nevertheless, be checked.

Even remote relatives in the clan are disqualified from marriage, and certain near biological "relatives" outside the clan
are actually preferred in marriage. This is particularly true
of a young man's mother's brother's daughter, a person called
a "cross-cousin" by anthropologists. This girl, who belongs
only to her mother's clan, cannot, therefore, belong to the
boy's clan. Her father, furthermore, is uncle to the boy, and,
in fact, is the man from whom the boy will one day inherit
wealth. What happier, more secure arrangement could there
be for a man than to have his daughter married to the young
man who will eventually succeed him? It apparently has
proved satisfactory to everyone for a long, long time, for it
remains the marriage which parents prefer for their children,
even though the frequency with which it occurs is diminishing.

These rules for intelligent mate selection have undoubtedly
always been broken to some degree. A good-looking cross-
cousin with all the other desirable qualities is not always easy
to find, and the more distant cross-cousins may prove to be
no improvement on the first. Nor are the rules so harshly enforced as to tie two incompatible young people into a marital
straitjacket just because their families prefer their marriage.
Indeed, it is frequently the young man himself who, having
first ascertained that she might be persuaded to consider him,
plants the rumor that he might be persuaded to consider her,
and their families then begin to work on the rumor for what

it may be worth. It is usually worth a lot, for a young man knows the rules and prefers to flout neither them nor the interests of his parents and family by threatening ridiculous, romantic nonsense with some flighty wench from a family of no standing. According to grandparents, there is more of this unorthodox marital foolishness in these modern, troublesome times when young men and women are losing respect for their elders and for the "real Ashanti," but even now it takes a thoroughly rebellious, sadly disorganized, or disappointingly modernized youngster to ignore completely the time-tested patterns.

All tests having been passed satisfactorily, the boy and the girl are married. The respective troths, for bride and groom, for bride's family and groom's family, are plighted in a quiet ceremony without benefit of either clergy or justice of the peace. Their services are dispensed with because marriages are not made in heaven and, therefore, no divine sanction is necessary; obligations to the ancestors, who must approve, and to the society, which must not be endangered, are fulfilled by the cautious inquiries and final approval of the two families. The crucial part of the ceremony consists of the giving of a small sum of money and various gifts by the family of the groom to that of the bride. The value of such payments is relatively small, frequently amounting in these fairly prosperous days to no more than $25. A groom's family, whether seeking or protecting prestige, may offer more, and a bride's family, for similar reasons, may demand more; a royal family automatically gives more and receives more, and a history of amicable relations between the families may prompt the exchange of greater wealth. It is rarely so large a sum, however, as to delay the marriage unduly.

Nor is the sum understood to represent a purchase of

property. A woman is by no means an animal to be bought and sold; she normally plays a subordinate role in the family life, but she has well-guarded personal rights which lift her out of the category of mere property. The payment of "bride wealth," as it is called, constitutes only a token of the agreement reached between her and her groom and between their families. In the giving and receiving of the gifts the young people and their families mutually pledge their faithfulness and support.

When this transaction has occurred before the witnessing members of both families, they are husband and wife joined together. After a small but festive party, the bride and groom retire quietly to his home, where she prepares a meal for him. For better or worse, they are married, and may they prosper, have many children, good health, and a long, peaceful life, protected by the venerable ancestors and the gracious gods.

Variations on these marriage themes have appeared in recent decades—among them is a relaxation of the incest rule against marriage with a fellow clansman related so distantly as to be unknown—but in Ashanti the old ideals are still respected and provide the major guides to behavior. The slight increase in alliances formed entirely without benefit of either clergy or families is viewed as a stupid, lamentable consequence of the general loosening of morals since the arrival of the British. Why, the elders ask, should a young woman risk her security by living with a man who refuses to prove his integrity by fulfilling his marriage customs? She cuts herself off from recourse to her family should he abandon her; he, likewise, cannot complain should she leave him. They have pledged nothing to each other; they can expect nothing from each other. The grayheads shake in contempt and in nostalgia for a better day. Nevertheless, many such marriages work out satisfactorily—just as they did "in the better days." Gray-heads have a tendency to forget.

Christian marriages are comparatively few in number. For one thing, they are more costly, entailing extra fees, entertainment, and gifts consonant with the Western standard of values that the church symbolizes. The churches have taken the position that they cannot perform a valid ceremony until the traditional Ashanti family obligations have been fulfilled, and, since their fulfillment constitutes a legitimate marriage, the church appears to have nothing essential to offer. There have been relatively few sufficiently Westernized families in Ashanti willing to undergo the additional expense of a marriage ceremony in the church, even though a certain amount of prestige may be gained by it. Still fewer believe deeply that a Christian, priestly ritual really provides something which the Ashanti family ritual does not. The large majority feel that the church ceremony is an unnecessary, alien imposition, intruding into a phase of life in which churchly religion is basically irrelevant.

A church wedding, furthermore, jeopardizes the future freedom of an individual to acquire a second or third wife. All the Christian churches forbid plural marriages and cite the New Testament injunctions against them. Ashanti Christians cite the Old Testament practice of polygyny in support of their custom and willingly accept the wages of their "sin." The penalties meted out by the churches include the denial of the sacraments and of all other rights of full church membership except those of attending and of contributing money. Under the circumstances, the penalties are not regarded as unduly harsh, and it is certainly far worse to take a pledge not to marry again nor to seek a divorce when there is likelihood of doing both. Thus, while there is nothing inherently wrong in a Christian marriage ceremony, few couples or families feel the need to have it performed.

Paradoxical as it may seen, matrilineal descent does not mean that Ashanti is a woman's world. It is not exactly a man's world, either, for an Ashanti woman does openly hold a few high cards in her hand and, of course, keeps a few others discreetly hidden. Nevertheless, when the time comes for decision making, it is the man who makes most of the decisions. The woman who tries to play a man's game may find herself suspected of sorcery, for her unladylike behavior bespeaks a "stronger soul," a manlike soul, which can easily get beyond her control and force her to commit acts dangerous to the health and life of the society. She may even admit to sorcery, for she, as well as anyone else, knows that a woman plays a subordinate role in Ashanti society. It is through the bodies of women that family, lineage, and clan membership is determined, but it is through the bodies and the minds of men that great things are achieved. The heroes of Ashanti are many, the heroines few.

The over-all status of a woman is reflected in the roles she plays as wife-and-mother. When she marries, her place of residence is determined by her husband to suit his purposes. Most marriages in Goaso are patrilocal; that is, the bride moves away from the home of her parents into that of her husband, who, by this time, is probably living with or near his mother's brother, although he may still be with his father. Thus separated from her family, she finds herself required to live with members of a number of families, that of her husband, that of her husband's married brothers' wives, perhaps that of her husband's father, and possibly those of her husband's father's matrilineal married nephews' wives, not to mention the families of the other wives of her husband, if he has already acquired them. The confusion actually is more apparent than real, but she does have to undergo the strain of assimilation to new family surroundings with their attendant anxieties.

If her husband prefers to allow her to remain in her own mother's home or in her brother's home or in another village, she is liable to suffer the anxieties of not knowing what he is up to while out of sight. Not that coresidence is crucial to the success of a marriage, for a wife remains secure in the bosom of her own family and never develops that feeling of tremendous dependence upon and exclusive possession of husbands which wives are thought to acquire in a Western society. The popularity of separate residence is most vividly to be seen at the dinner hour, when many small children scurry through the lanes of the town, their mobile bodies topped by immobile heads on which rest pots or pans containing the meal their mother has prepared over her own hearth for her husband, who will eat it in the company of the men in his own home. In most cases, however, the woman does live with her husband in his home. Here a wife has numerous duties, some of which she performs co-operatively with the other women of the household. In addition to caring for her own children, she may also serve as a substitute mother for the children of the other women, including those belonging to the other wives of her husband. She may also be called upon, now and then, to be a mother to her sister's children, whose name for her is "mother." The women of the household may also participate co-operatively in the preparation of meals, and in the eating of meals they always join with each other and with the children, while the men enjoy one another's company in a separate section of the courtyard.

Meet My Families

Cooking the main meal—and it should be ready by about 4:30 P.M., to follow immediately after her husband's bath—is merely one of the chores of the woman's day, for she has been busy since 6:00 A.M., when she arose to accompany her children and the other women to the river for the day's water supply. Frequently going without breakfast—breakfast only produces lethargy; the lazy always eat breakfast—she walks to the farm of her husband, perhaps a mile or two from town, where she spends a good portion of the day until 2:00 P.M. or so, weeding, replanting, harvesting food for the evening meal, and gathering firewood. This is not a completely onerous chore, for at least part of the land she works is her own, a gift from her husband at the time of her marriage. The garden vegetables and fruits she grows on her acre or two of land are hers by indisputable right; she uses them to feed her family, and any surplus she produces may be sold in the market at whatever profit she may make. And the profit is solely hers; her husband asks no questions.

Accompanying her to the farm is her youngest child, fastened snugly to her back if he is yet too young to keep up with his mother's graceful strides. If he is too young to toddle, he will stay in his secure cache, bending and swaying with the movement of the working back to which he is tied, his head lolling backward and flopping sideward as he takes his naps. If he cries, a deft loosening of the knot holding the wraparound, a quick shift of the hip, and a supporting arm get him where he wants to be, at his mother's breast. He sucks and stops crying. And in a few minutes she is back to work.

Nearby are the other women of the household, in-laws and perhaps cowives, working, as she, in their gardens or on the farms of their husbands, for their men often have ownership rights to the same or adjacent farms. As they work, the trees of the surrounding forest may tremble to the derisive songs of the cowives. "That child you think you carry in your belly is not a child; it's just a tumor." "Ayyy; turn to your weeding, you useless, childless woman." Or the trees may sigh that one man should have married two such compatible, amicable women.

Early in the afternoon the women finish their work and return home with some of the fruits of their labor, like the heavy head loads of plantain and firewood—and the baby. Such loads as these, weighing perhaps upward of forty pounds, are balanced delicately but securely upon a small cloth pad atop the head. Many a woman is skillful enough to maneuver a squawling infant back to front for breast feeding on demand without spilling the load or breaking stride.

Reaching home before her husband, she warms the water for his bath and starts to clean the vegetables and pound the fufu. This dish, the principal ingredient in any successful meal, is prepared from boiled yam, cassava, or plantain pounded to a dumplinglike consistency in a large mortar. At three each afternoon all Ashanti echoes to the thud, thud, thud of the heavy pestle, thumping out the rhythm of this staple food, as Ashanti wives, aided by their children, work to fill their hungry husbands. The woman boils the meat stew, checks and bathes the children, and readies herself and the household for his return from the farm. The palm wine should be brought out, too, for the gourd he took with him to enliven an otherwise monotonous day of toil will be empty. And so will he.

The wife puts in a big day. But that is how things are for women. There is no feminist movement in Ashanti; not yet, anyway, although the rumblings of complaint and rearrangement can faintly be heard among the more educated, more

Westernized women of the city, some of whom have entered the professions of education, journalism, and medicine. In any society a woman learns early and often what is normally expected of her in the division of labor, and she comes to do it with little or no thought about the justice or injustice of it or about a possible redistribution of the work. It seems as proper for an Ashanti wife to carry the heavy basket from the farm as for an American wife to burden her husband with the packages.

The amount of work performed by a woman is one of the reasons why few women oppose their husbands' polygynous marriages. It is also one of the reasons why men favor polygynous marriages. One wife among several finds her own work load reduced, and their husband finds the work output of his immediate family increased. Because their increased production increases the wealth of the husband's extended family, that group also approves the acquisition of more than one wife. So everyone is satisfied. Indeed, many women so favor the idea of having an extra wife or two in the family that they encourage their husbands to bestir themselves and find some, and most husbands, if they can afford it, are only too happy to oblige. Having more than one wife confers prestige and more offspring in addition to increasing the wealth and reducing the toil of previous wives who have served faithfully and are deserving of a more leisurely life. Frequently, though not necessarily, the first wife assumes a senior role in the family and directs the domestic affairs of the entire household. But this in no way demeans the position of the other wives, who feel not at all inferior to wives in monogamous marriages and who, in fact, may justifiably exhibit some slight pride in having won the favor of a man capable of investing in extra wives.

There is jealousy, of course, in many polygynous households, but the dexterous avoidance of favoritism by an astute, sympathetic husband is usually sufficient to keep this under control, if not to suppress it entirely. The sensible husband sets up a rotating system by which each of his wives lives with him for a week or two, sleeping with him, preparing his meals, caring for his laundry, conversing with him, and making him extremely happy. When her week is up, she returns to her home or to her rooms until all the others have enjoyed their turn.

If this system seems to fall somewhat short of an American girl's dream of an idyllic marriage, she might just remind herself that it may not fall quite so short of an American boy's dream of an idyllic marriage. More importantly, she should recall that few Ashanti, married or unmarried, regard a mate as an exclusive, private possession or marriage as a divine institution created for the satisfaction of a couple of people, their few children, and for the glory of the gods. Marriages, to be sure, are not exactly loveless. Young people are permitted to express their preferences, and these are likely to reflect the warm emotions of "love" rather than the cold calculations of family welfare planning. Fights for "love," though uncommon, sometimes occur. Furthermore, many examples of ideal marriages may be found, marriages which have endured for life because of the lasting, mutual affection between husband and wife and children. It is an affection, however, tempered by a respectful distance which the proper wife maintains between herself and her husband. On the whole, the steady, cooling wind of long-range realism keeps the emotional temperatures well regulated at all times. And so, in the absence of a romantic tradition, polygyny becomes completely feasible, even desirable. Polygynous life can be beautiful.

Not all married life, however, is beautiful, and the Ashanti make reasonable allowances through divorce for those who fail to make a go of it. Of the accepted grounds for divorce incompatibility is probably one of the most frequent, and couples can separate by mutual consent if relations between them are strained beyond the point of reconciliation. The quarrelsome or nagging wife, the profligate, drunken, or repeatedly promiscuous husband, the man who fails to support his wife and children, the woman who fails to care for her household, the adulteress—all these may find themselves mateless one day. But almost as many divorces result from a single cause, the failure to have children, as from these others. For barrenness or sterility robs the individuals and their families of that strength and joy in human beings which all desire intensely.

Divorce is not easily won, since marriage is regarded as much a union of families as it is a union of individuals. At best divorce is a poor solution to problems which ought to be solved in such a way as to maintain a stable family and harmonious interfamily relations. Unless the reason is failure to produce children, representatives of both families and arbitrators selected by them protect the interests of all the parties by attempting to persuade the couple to reconcile their differences. If they fail to do so, the arbitrators determine whose is the greater fault. If it is the man's, the bride wealth his family paid at the time of the marriage is not returned. If it is the woman's fault, the bride wealth is returned, and the stigma of failure is placed upon the guilty. When the woman is convicted of adultery she has offended the ancestors and the gods, and in her confession she must name her lovers, who, if convicted, must pay a fee to the aggrieved husband for their misconduct. By their acts they

have ridiculed the man and slighted the rights which the ancestors have bequeathed to husbands, and it is only fair that
they make and he receive recompense. A single misstep may
not justify divorce, but repetition leads to the unhappy consequence.

It is usual for a woman in a divorce to return to her family
with her daughters and with sons still in their infancy or
early childhood. The father, however, may choose to keep his
sons with him or to receive them back from their mother
after they have reached school age. In any event he is likely
to remain identified with and affectionate toward his sons
throughout their lives, even though in late adolescence they
will return to their mother and the mother's family, of which
they become increasingly important members.

The Ashanti feel that divorce, though recognized in early
times, has increased in frequency since the arrival of the Europeans and the consequent shift in social values. Wives who
are attracted to some of the amenities of the new way
of life and are becoming more independent economically
through the acquisition of cocoa-producing lands are apt to
become more contentious. In consequence, more and more
people are found who have had more than one wife or husband in sequence.

The absence of records makes difficult an estimate of divorce rates, but it is more than likely that the rate in Ashanti
slightly exceeds that of the United States. A redeeming feature
of this situation, however, is the way in which the organization of Ashanti family life minimizes the harmful effects of
the "broken family." Children of divorced parents are not
forced to walk an emotion-splitting tightrope between two
single, separate parents. Since their birth they have been
members of a large extended family replete with human rela-

tionships of an intimate, satisfying sort. The divorce of their parents in no way disrupts the children's family identification, and, while they may regret the partial loss of a parent, they remain secure members of an affectionate family group. If one family "breaks," the other, larger, more important family remains whole.

5. Learning to Live

Birth into a culture such as this is a precarious event, so precarious that perhaps half of all children born die before they reach the age of three years. Because accurate, scientific knowledge of the causes of infant death is not yet widespread, defense of these tender lives is still largely a religious one, using rituals and charms. Religion is also called upon to explain the death of children who do not reach puberty. One can never be certain that a person was really meant to be born until he has proved it by living long enough to assume adult roles. For the person has his origin in another and spiritual world and must be completely ready to adopt this existence before he arrives on earth. If he is not ready he makes an early retirement, quite possibly to return again in another birth at another time. The death of an infant or child is mourned but little—although his parents and family feel great sorrow—for Death, who revels in pain, should not be encouraged by displays of grief to seize still other young lives.

For all the dangers attendant upon birth, there is no lack of desire to have children. Among the more unhappy people in Goaso is a man who is childless. He has had six consecutive wives but no children, and in spite of his six failures he is making a seventh attempt.

The Ashanti believe that within the body of the mother

her blood and the blood of her mother's family are given the form of a new human life when it receives the soul of the father. The soul of the father is the soul he received from his father at conception and this has protected and prospered him through all his years. Thus a child represents the complementary unity of two lines of descent joined together in his person. The blood from which he is formed is matrilineal, and he will always belong to his mother's family; but the soul which gives life to the blood is patrilineal, received from his father and from his father's father. Although he will never "belong" to his father in the same sense that he "belongs" to his mother, the child and his family will always remember who it is that has given him life and whose soul he carries within him. This soul goes with him throughout his life; when he marries it will extend its care over his wife and will mingle with her blood to form a new child, who, in turn, will live and grow to transmit the soul to still another generation.

When a woman is ready to deliver her child, she goes to the home of her mother, for it is of her mother's blood and into her mother's family that the child is born. Here, in modest seclusion from men and attended by the elderly, experienced women of her family, she gives birth. The tension of those first few postnatal moments is tremendous, and the relief explosive when the infant announces that he has arrived to be with his family. A baby's life is such a tentative thing, however, that seven days ensue before he receives his name. Then, if he has passed this crucial period and, by staying alive, has signified that he intends to remain alive, he receives his "day-name" from the day of the week on which he was born. From then on he bears this name, which is the name of his soul; for the soul, inherited from the father, is also identified

74

with the day on which it made its appearance into the world.

If, aided by the tender ministrations of his mother, his maternal grandmother and aunts, and by the gods and ancestors who attempt to protect him from danger, the infant survives for another week, his father leisurely and proudly strolls through the village cradling in his arms this wonderfully helpless symbol of his good fortune for all to see. On that day, or shortly thereafter, the infant receives other names, "strong-names," in honor of great men and great deeds in Ashanti or in the family, or other names of paternal ancestors whose likeness is seen or felt in this child. Ancestors have been known to return again from their ancestral world, reincarnate in children, and this strong, healthy child may be a well-remembered great-grandfather on his father's side.

Government or mission medical technicians and midwives are called upon to substitute for the elderly female family member in delivering many babies these days, but a shortage of facilities in out-of-the-way places and a strong desire for the psychological security found only in the bosom of the family prevent many expectant mothers from making full use of the government or mission medical dispensaries. Many women seek modern prenatal and postnatal care for themselves and their infants, but weaning them away from their maternal homes for the birth itself is a slower process. The advantages of the relatively sterile delivery room and its trained but impersonal, white-garbed attendants are not self-evident to persons who value highly the experienced wisdom of personally interested, if unsterile, kinfolk. The delivery room will prevail, but not quite yet.

Early childhood is a characteristically carefree time, largely void of harsh punishments and filled with mothering from many of the mothers who live in the household, from the father, and from the grandfather. Breast feeding comes on demand, and the infant's mother or somebody's mother is generally nearby to answer the wailing commands. Weaning occurs sometime during the second year, preferably when the next child is born, which, ideally, is about the time the previous child reaches two years of age. If there is no competition for the breasts, and mother's milk is still available, it may continue to be part of the diet for even longer periods. When the change comes, it occurs over a span of perhaps two weeks, and from then on the child's menu is identical with that of adults, filled with starchy items and woefully deficient in proteins and energy foods.

Milk in Ashanti comes only in human breasts or in cans of condensed milk from Europe, because the tsetse fly and the sleeping sickness this vicious insect carries destroy the bovine producers, and sheep and goat milks are reserved for infant sheep and goats. Because canned milk is new and expensive, and because human milk is obviously in short supply, children just don't drink much milk. Besides, everyone, including two-year-old children, loves fufu. It has been loved for generations and its inherent inadequacies have not yet been demonstrated to Ashanti's satisfaction; nor have adequate alternatives been developed.

Growing children are introduced into adult work responsibilities as they become physically capable of assuming them. Sons become more and more the subjects of fatherly training in the skills and arts of making a living, of family and political administration, and of religion. Daughters learn the roles of womanhood from their mothers and the other women of the household, while all participate in those common tasks of farming which fall to everyone.

Among the most desired goals of womanhood is the bearing

and rearing of children, a role for which practice in play begins early in childhood. Sometimes the play-doll fondly tucked into the wrap-around dress of the practice-mother has pinkish skin and has been manufactured in England. This is of no moment, for to the brown-skinned little girl a baby is a baby. And so the brown girl fondles and feeds and cleans and punishes and loves her pink doll. Frequently she has a real baby, a brother or sister or cousin to tend. When her own child is born, she has little to learn.

The dark, gleaming bodies of young boys and girls are often wet with the cool pleasures of play in the pool or stream. Ashanti girls can always be distinguished from Ashanti boys by the strings of colorful "waist beads" they wear, for the nakedness of girls and women is modestly hidden by a cloth attached to bright beads which encircle their loins. Boys and men are modest, too, but the etiquette of modesty doesn't decree any covering until later in childhood.

Children, too, perform numerous chores. In the early dawn it is time to get water from the stream; in the late afternoon it is time to pound fufu and deliver the evening meal to father or uncle; and in between there is work to do on the farm, errands to run, and light loads to carry. Small boys, trailing along behind a group of men and balancing big chairs or stools inverted on their heads, so that fathers can sit in comfort when they wish, may be seen in almost any village at any time of day. And if the boys keep their ears open and their mouths closed as they serve the men they will learn the wisdom of their elders and so be prepared for the day when their sons will carry their chairs and learn their wisdom.

When not working there is time for spontaneous play in the lanes, fields, and forest, for soccer football, and for games of cowboys and Indians. Since the advent of the western

77

movie in Ashanti, hordes of small, black-skinned Sioux braves have galloped through Ashanti towns, their paper-feathered headdresses and war whoops striking terror into the hearts of the small, black-skinned cowboys. Meanwhile, for the girls, there is always more laundry to be done in families as large as these and in a climate as warm and humid as this. The sometimes unwilling girls are reminded that domestic skills never lessen their chances of a superior marriage. Most girls reluctantly agree, and all boys agree absolutely.

Until the personalities of children are revealed in play and conversation, perhaps their most noticeable feature is their distended abdomens, the result of malnutrition or of the intestinal diseases from which most persons frequently suffer. The round stomachs disappear gradually during childhood, to be replaced—for the same reasons—by the low energy level which continues through the rest of life for most persons. Still, the boy of four years who carries a protruding navel, his "snuffbox," in the circumference of his circular abdomen is not necessarily lacking in physical or mental agility. He may be nuisance enough at home for his mother to appreciate and pamper his desire to get on to school. Too young to enroll, he may dress prematurely in his school uniform and trudge up the road to the schoolhouse to listen to the lessons. It will not be surprising if in fifteen years or so he is registered at Oxford University or at Columbia University, without his stomach, with the experience of a thorough preparatory education at the University College of Ghana, with the pride and charm of manner of an African people for whom etiquette is the *sine qua non*, and with all the aggressive eagerness of a hopeful people who firmly believe they have a bright and independent future.

A large proportion of the children of school age in any

78

town now spend most of their days acquiring literate skills and thus avoid some of the farm-work regimen of their parents. In Goaso, as elsewhere in Ashanti, schooling is considered to be more valuable for boys than for girls, and few of the latter achieve more than a modicum of literate skills. The history book's Wellington at Waterloo is a far cry from an Ashanti household, and as for modern politics and most occupations, they are for men. Still, many girls do attend school for a few years and are the happier—or unhappier—for it. Even for the large majority of boys schooling ends with the completion of six years or less of study, and the greatest percentage of those who cannot or do not wish to continue resume what has in recent years become the rewarding occupation of cocoa farming. In this underschooled country, attendance has not been compulsory, but the advantages of a formal education have been so universally recognized by parents and children alike that there is a clamor for schools even in remote villages. The provision of teachers and facilities for six years of classes constitutes a major problem for a government which already devotes a major portion of its budget to education. Most towns impose taxes upon themselves to furnish the buildings and supplies for instruction, and citizens freely donate the necessary labor.

Goaso's children have a choice of two schools, one of ten grades supervised by the Roman Catholic Church, the other of six grades supervised by the Methodist Church. So great is the demand for these schools that the children of many other communities, lacking in comparable facilities, flock to Goaso to live with their lineage members and gain the means to what is presumed to be assured future success.

Unfortunately for the aspirations of these children and their parents, there is even less room at the top in nonindustrialized Ghana than there is in the United States, and the plateau of relative success which lies below the top is even more difficult of access than it is in America. There are numerous frustrated holders of school achievement certificates of one kind or another in the Goaso area who have been to school and now can find nowhere else to go. Fortunately, western Ashanti does offer at least partially satisfying rewards to those young men who become or remain cocoa farmers. It does not, therefore, face directly the problem of the restless, literate student who holds a diploma and who wants badly to exploit his superior qualifications but who can find few economic opportunities commensurate with what he considers to be his real worth.

Elsewhere in Ashanti, and particularly in the large towns and cities, this growing group of dissatisfied, educated young men poses a social problem of major importance. Vocal and active in politics, they are in the vanguard of those groups seeking more rapid economic and social change. Their desires are pitched high; the opportunities for fulfilling them are still pitched low. Inevitably, this kind of frustration leads to aggression against any convenient target, and British colonialism has provided a big one. Goaso, for the most part, has avoided the more violent agitation, because it is removed from the populous centers of administration and power and because it can still offer adequately attractive incomes to its relatively less well-educated people.

Schoolteachers, ideally, are trained for about a total of twelve years, including two years of teachers' college. Such persons generally serve as headmasters or upper-grade teachers in local schools and provide the leadership for the educational programs. Most of the teachers, however, are young men, many of whom have had no more than ten years of schooling themselves, some of them even less than that. All have a herculean task of teaching numerous subjects to too-numerous pupils in inadequate quarters with few teaching supplies and too-small salaries.

If the American school program cries for more of everything except pupils, the plight of a comparatively poor, previously unschooled country can easily be imagined. But everywhere there is growth and potential strength, and even now a trickle of Goaso students is reaching the top level of Ghana education, the University College of Ghana, an excellent college associated in the British university system with the University of London. A few Goaso boys have even gone on to university or other specialized training programs in England and the United States.

During the first two years of school teaching is done in one of the dialects of the Twi language group, of which the Ashanti language is a member. Many young people have become literate in this language, even though the literature is unfortunately small. Progressively more and more instruction in English is given after the second year, and by the time a pupil reaches the terminal elementary grade, after ten years, he is adequately, though not expertly, literate in English. An unfortunately large number of students drop out of school after the sixth year, however, and adequate communication in English in rural areas is still possible only with a small minority of the people. The English of the minority which does finish ten years of study constitutes, as may be expected, a new, fascinating dialect of the language not always completely comprehensible to the native speaker of English. Almost any town of the size and status of Goaso, nevertheless, has a dozen persons able to carry on a complex conversation in highly competent English.

In the absence of trained teaching personnel and adequate equipment for instruction in agriculture and other technical subjects, and because of the traditional bent of English education, a classical school curriculum has been maintained in the elementary and secondary schools. Reading, writing, arithmetic and mathematics, Western literature, the history of Western civilizations, languages, and religion form the core courses; music, hygiene, and domestic arts are frequently included in the earlier years, physical and some social sciences in the later years. Nice subjects, they are, and each one justifiable on one ground or another, some of them on excellent grounds indeed. Perfectly taught and perfectly learned, they would create a generation of healthy gentlemen and scholars who could sing European music, cook vitaminized dishes, and recite the most revered traditions of the Western democracies. Parts of the curriculum have even been intellectually dangerous to the colonial *status quo*. Wellington at Waterloo is not a particularly subversive individual, to be sure, but Gandhi, Lincoln, and a considerable number of Englishmen add nothing to the passivity of colonial Africans while quickening democratic ideals. The British have certainly helped to speed their own departure from Ghana through at least some of their educational policies.

Many teachers, youthful and insecure in their own knowledge, are forced to rely upon the methods of repeated drill and monotonous repetition in their classroom techniques. The resemblance of rote memorization to integrated learning is remote, and, while probably no educational system will ever score 100 per cent on a test of effectiveness, few Ashanti school systems even remotely threaten to do so. Even the teaching of "Western social principles" is not without its disadvantages. Many social principles of the Western world

82

are, by themselves, little more than fantasies when taught in an economic setting which is insufficiently developed to permit their realization. Many of the Ashanti who think at all critically about such matters feel that the curriculum is insufficiently adjusted to modern Ashanti life and that greater emphasis should be placed on "practical," technological knowledge. They would like more instruction in technical, commercial, industrial, and professional skills. As national consciousness grows, furthermore, they express the desire for greater emphasis upon the "principles which have made Ashanti great."

Still, there is no need to carp unduly about Ghana education. In contrast to many parts of the colonial world, the British have here worked to provide schools on all levels of advancement for at least a substantial minority of the population. Those within the system realize many of its shortcomings more keenly than does the naturally critical observer. Besides, the system, for all its faults, is getting results. Despite the relative absence of those social characteristics which are usually correlated with Western democracy—urbanization, industrialism, a large middle class, and a substantial, informed, free vote—the schools are working changes in the society.

The schools do make a difference. They are able to make a difference, in part because of what they are, in part because the material and social environment in which they have been placed is not antagonistic to them or to what they teach. Man does not live by fufu alone, but he needs plenty of it; he has it in Ashanti. Nor is Ghana, on the whole, as economically depressed as most of the underdeveloped areas of the world; the country can support a broad network of schools. In addition, man in most of Ghana, including Ashanti, has long had a social tradition which includes many democratic elements.

Although hardly a model of Western, representative democracy, society in this part of the misnamed "Dark Continent" has long contained much that is compatible with liberal social institutions. In this setting the schools, even as they are, achieve results. At a later time, in a more adequate world, they will be more effective, but it is difficult now to conceive of any considerable increase in their effectiveness without tremendous expansion, insupportable in the immediate present, of the quantity, quality, and cost of education.

Christian missions founded the first Ghana schools and the Christian denominations have retained most of the supervision of the local school systems. The Ghana government, however, strongly influences over-all policy, sets standards of accreditation, and pays most of the bills. Local communities also support their schools through special, self-imposed tax levies. The result has been a semipublic, semireligious school program in which the administering denominations have tended to guard their prerogatives zealously and to engage in jurisdictional clashes over the right to maintain schools in local communities. Here and there in Ashanti, Protestant missions have united their educational activities in unified schools, but many towns still support separate Roman Catholic and Protestant denominational schools on the elementary and secondary levels.

Nearly all of the denominations with missionary enterprises in Ghana have discovered that mere oratory and argument lack sufficient power to persuade people of their fallen nature and of the regeneration which comes through Christian ritual, theology, and morals. Schools, on the other hand, have proved highly persuasive, and the banging of the school gong has converted far more pagans than the tolling of the church bell. As a result, school gong and church bell frequently are one and the same.

Foreseeing the withering of what they consider to be their primary function, the religious function—because of the abolition of their schools or their incorporation into a secular state system—denominations have struggled to preserve their lives through the preservation of their schools in local communities. Many missionaries have thus found most of their time consumed by the tasks of superintending school affairs. Rattling journeys by truck over abominable roads, weeklong treks on foot along forest trails, leaky roofs, indigent students, complaints about teacher salaries, cash shortages, and unbalanced accounts—these and other trials call for the best in faith, hope, and c'arity. Most missionaries appear to have adequate amounts of all three. But the tests of these virtues are severe enough to make a furlough back home welcome, and the hope of a furlough must be counted among the motivations for the performance of a difficult task.

Goaso is one of those numerous towns in which two schools vie with each other for enrollment. The Roman Catholic school, with superior facilities and more numerous classes, has outdistanced the older but less well-financed, more meagerly staffed Methodist school. The former has nearly 250 students distributed unevenly through its ten grades, in inverse proportion to the level of advancement. About a dozen boys, in their final year, hope to pass the examinations which will qualify them for secondary school. The Methodist school teaches about 90 students in six grades. Six or seven harried teachers "handle" the Catholic school, three the Methodist, and the latter are at least as harried as the former, for they work in a single large church sanctuary as compared to the six separate though crowded classrooms available to the Catholics. Altogether, the schools provide something less than a completely edifying experience, but those who teach, those who study, and those who send their children to be taught want only more and better schooling.

Of such stuff are the materials of rural Ashanti childhood, the stuff of which modern adults are made. But before they can taste the ripe fruits of old age and go in peace to the ancestral world they must step gingerly through a world which poses numerous threats to health and life, threats which have not yet been satisfactorily contained.

6. Matters of Life and Death

Prayers for long life and numerous children are uttered daily in Goaso, and well they may be, for a lamentable number of these prayers are unsatisfactorily answered. Births are numerous enough, but the infants who reach the age of three years may consider themselves fortunate, for nearly half of their contemporaries fail to do so. Once through that crucial period of infancy and tender childhood, the outlook is fair for a life of perhaps forty to forty-five years, but few people need bother to make plans for many of the years beyond fifty. Some, of course, attain a really old age, but the hazards of dietary deficiencies and tropical illnesses are numerous and usually insurmountable.

In the absence of scientific knowledge about disease and its causes, ill-health is generally traced to the activity of supernatural beings, gods, ancestors, lesser spirits of one sort or another, or to sorcery. Because the causes are supernatural, it is logical to call upon religious specialists in the supernatural to diagnose illnesses and to rely upon supernatural treatments for curing them. Although the people of Goaso are supplied with an overabundance of nonscientific assumptions about health and disease, they are consistent and logical enough to use their nonscientific religion as a means of adjusting to what otherwise would be a psychologically shattering predicament. Indeed, the Ashanti are as logical—and as illogical—in their thinking as anyone anywhere; the differences between them and scientifically oriented Westerners lie basically in the religious and magical assumptions about reality from which their thinking proceeds.

Good health, to be sure, is not solely a religious concern for the Ashanti; if it were, there would be no Ashanti to write about. Practically all these people have a stock of home remedies with which to treat ills, and probably most of these have scientific validity at least equal to that of the home remedies and patent nostrums still popular in America. Wounds are bandaged and broken bones set and bound; stimulants and sedatives may be found in the traditional pharmacopoeia. Emetics and laxatives are taken in profusion at the first signs of illness; they may not help much, but, on the other hand, they may be just what any doctor would order. It is more than likely that long, bitter experience has produced some valid cures, and the application of soothing heat and massage are examples of unquestionably effective therapy.

Many such simple treatments, especially those for injuries rather than for illnesses, are considered as just treatments, without any religious element in them. Most treatments, however, are regarded as aspects of a total treatment which does include religious ingredients. The distinction between what Americans might consider to be physical or scientific cures and spiritual or religious cures is not usually made in Ashanti. Heat and massage are usually understood to frighten or rub out the offending evil force causing the pain. Lacking scientific theories, the Ashanti rely upon supernatural theories of medi-

cine, and their identification of religious and physical prescriptions is quite in keeping with their theories.

They have plenty to theorize about, for Ghana, while no
longer living up to its old, ominous name, "the white man's
grave," remains a comparatively unhealthful place when judged
by the best European or American standards. That name,
incidentally, only slightly exaggerates the conditions of existence prior to the second decade of this century. The toll
among early missionaries, traders, government officers, and
soldiers pushing into the bush was discouraging; malaria was
a particularly vicious murderer in the days when preventive
measures were uncertain and the conditions of work made it
tempting to skip the tedious treatment. Europeans did not
have the chance to skip many treatments. That the killer did
not equally decimate the African population was due to the
partial immunity or resistance built up in a population in
which nearly everyone had malaria at one time or another.
Malaria did, however, account for many African premature
deaths, and it still does.

Certain of the diseases peculiar to temperate climates or to
overcrowded, unsanitary city areas are not present in tropical,
rural Ashanti. The danger of violent death or injury from traffic or household accidents also is greatly reduced. It is possible
that the personal damage per vehicle is greater in Ashanti than
in the United States, but there are not enough vehicles or other
death-dealing gadgets to necessitate perpetual safety campaigns. The disadvantages, nevertheless, outweigh the advantages, and the well-protected man in the Western world can
expect to live about twenty years longer than his Ashanti contemporary.

Foremost among the health problems in Ashanti and
throughout Ghana are those caused by nutritional deficiencies,

especially in proteins and energy foods. Although the generally low economic productivity of Africans is often attributed by white men to sheer laziness, inborn and ineradicable, and indicative of gross moral turpitude, the actual causes are much more prosaic. Current research is indicating that such unmoral factors as traditional work patterns and non-Western attitudes toward the value of work, as well as the sheer lack of physical energy due to faulty diets and food habits, all conspire to reduce production.

In addition to the deficiencies of their primarily starchy diet, numerous intestinal diseases afflict practically all Ashanti, although important steps to reduce their toll are being taken by government agencies, particularly in urban areas. Tapeworms, roundworms, and amebic and other dysenteries are common. As if these were not enough, a long inventory of other tropical diseases can be added to the debilitating factors in Ashanti life. Besides the ubiquitous malaria, there is trypanosomiasis (sleeping sickness), yellow fever, bilharzia and several other parasite infections; these are but the more common. And as if these were not enough, the inventory can be extended by almost all the diseases found in temperate climates; the common cold, pneumonia, and tuberculosis, smallpox, chicken pox, diphtheria, whooping cough, and others. Almost everyone has been afflicted with yaws in childhood, and leg ulcers are common throughout life. To these may be added those which are diagnosed as "just another tropical fever" for want of adequate knowledge. Nor do these exhaust the discouraging list.

Lest even this brief description eliminate Ghana from future travel itineraries, it should be pointed out that the control of these diseases by medical science has increased to such a point that most normally healthy Europeans or Americans can spend a long period of time even in the bush with little more than the annoyance of the inevitable diarrhea. This minor ailment, furthermore, is not a source of excessive embarrassment to the sufferer, for practically everyone else is just recovering or just coming down with an attack.

Germs, viruses, protein and vitamin deficiencies, and the rest of the scientifically determined causes of disease do not figure in Ashanti medical theory. Nor do Ashanti references to "small, invisible animals" constitute an awareness of the germ as a carrier of sickness. To most Americans a germ may be only a "small, invisible animal," but there is at least a qualified group of scientists in America who can identify a germ for what it is. There is no such trained class of people in the field of traditional Ashanti medicine; those modern Ashanti who know about germs have been trained in modern, scientific rather than in traditional medicine. Uninformed persons still look upon the little animals and most other causes of sickness as agents of some supernatural ill will.

Among the traditional explanations of disease is destiny, a kind of fatalistic belief that before his birth the victim contracted to suffer his misery in exchange for some advantage in life, such as being born ahead of schedule or reaping unusual wealth. Illnesses may be attributed to the retribution of ancestors who have been angered by human indifference to them or by some breach of traditional morality. The gods may be similarly insulted and provoked into extracting justice through the infliction of pain. A frequent source of illness is sorcery, performed by some person, often a female member of the extended family, who has acquired supernatural power, either accidentally or purposely, to inflict harm.

After folk remedies have failed to solve the health problem in its initial stages, the time comes to consult with a qualified medico-religious specialist in order to determine which of these or other similar supernatural causes may be responsible. The test of a specialist's qualifications is his known effectiveness in treating illness; if he has proved his ability to communicate with the supernatural in such a way as to diagnose and prescribe cures, he is obviously the man to consult.

This method of handling disease is unsatisfactory to members of a science-minded community, and the effectiveness of treatment in an Ashanti community is also unsatisfactory to an objective observer. The Ashanti mortality rate is high, the life expectancy relatively low. But subjectively the method is not without satisfactions for members of an Ashanti community. It satisfies, in the main, because it provides an explanation of what is happening. Disease, a universal problem, needs explanations and treatments, and each society develops what appears to it to be reasonable explanations and treatments. Not to do so would result in an utterly intolerable existence. Not to do so is, in fact, unthinkable, and in the absence of scientific realism a society thinks up answers to such crucial questions. Without more adequate alternative answers, it is not surprising that the traditional answers persist in quieting the fears which inevitably accompany illness.

The medico-religious specialist—often called witch doctor or medicine man by the Western skeptic—stands a fair chance, furthermore, of guessing right on his prognosis, regardless of the treatment he prescribes. A patient, after all, has just three possibilities: he can die, he can recover completely, or he can remain sick. Since the ultimate question is one of life or death and since the Goaso specialist has a backlog of shrewd, common-sense observations on which to draw, he can make a well-informed prediction. Then consider the effect on a doctor's prestige if his prediction of death fails to materialize. His reputation is established, for he has demonstrated his ability to defeat the seemingly overwhelming opposition of supernatural ill will. It takes an extremely unlucky specialist to fail abysmally in his career.

There are some occupational hazards in the medico-religious profession, but by and large they are not staggering, and with ordinary luck and slightly better than ordinary insight most specialists have made a go of it. There are, furthermore, plenty of explanations for failure, since the curative capabilities of supernatural good will are not regarded as all-powerful. They may, at times, prove inferior to those of ill will, and no stigma attaches to the unsuccessful practitioner unless he persistently loses his patients. Such utter failures occur so infrequently as to confirm and support faith in both the profession and its familiar, traditional techniques.

Still other satisfactions grow out of this view of health and medicine, satisfactions which contribute to the mental and social health of the community. The explanations for many illnesses are found in some antisocial behavior on the part either of the victim or of some persons closely related to him in the family or community. To cure such ills, therefore, requires the righting of some social wrong. In any area of the world where persons are acutely aware of their dependence upon all the other members of their community, where a breach in social relations threatens almost the very survival of the group, there must be numerous devices for maintaining the solidarity of the group. In Ashanti, therefore, where existence itself is often precarious, health and medicine become means for detecting threats to social unity and for reestablishing those harmonious social relationships which are essential to life.

93

Perhaps foremost among these threats to the unity of the group are witches and sorcerers. For all the generally prevailing harmony in any group of people, occasions do arise in which hostility and conflict threaten the harmony and solidarity of the group. When these occur, and when they are accompanied, as they often are, by certain kinds of prolonged illness or by the barrenness of women or economic bad luck, it seems obvious to trace them to the nefarious operations of a supernatural spirit of ill will which has wormed its way into some member of the group. More often than not, the sorcerer when identified turns out to be a nonconformist whose behavior in some respect deviates too far from the social ideal, who poses a threat to the normal majority of persons who live as they should. Whether or not the accusation of sorcery is justified—and many of the accused are actually persuaded of their guilt—the public exposure of the antisocial person and the exercising of the evil spirit brings a general feeling of relief and well-being to the victim, to his attacker, and to the whole society. And when people are enjoying peace of mind they stand a much improved chance of regaining soundness of body.

This supernatural theory of medicine helps to reinforce mental and social health is still another way. The practitioner may divine that the cause of certain diseases is to be found in the punitive actions of gods or ancestors. Now, these good spirits are not testy creatures who project sickness indiscriminately upon the innocent; they express their anger usually when there is sickness in the body politic which needs curing. As defenders of the right and protectors of the people, they are quick to react to any appearance of antisocial conduct which threatens their children, and they frequently do so by visiting illness upon the offenders, a chastisement which, like any social ill, unfortunately affects the innocent along with the guilty. Diagnosis of the illness, then, is largely a diagnosis of a social offense, and the curing of the illness requires the righting of a social wrong. When viewed in this light, the threat of suffering becomes a powerful incentive for moral behavior, and the cure of suffering becomes a sign that the gods and ancestors are pleased once more, that immorality has been excised, and the whole society restored to moral good health. Not all illness has this social significance, but much of it is turned in this way to the service of the emotional solidarity and the moral integrity of the community.

However inadequate Ashanti medical theory may seem to most Americans or Europeans in the mid-twentieth century, the prescientific explanations of the Western world less than two centuries ago differed but little from those of Ashanti. Today, new theories, scientific theories, have been introduced into Ashanti by the British, and a process of unlearning the old and learning the new has begun. If the acceptance of modern medical science comes more slowly in Goaso than in America, it is because the new approach to problems of health and medicine is too unfamiliar, too radically different from the old.

Most Ashanti, furthermore, see no reason why scientific methods need completely supplant the traditional methods. The worth of the new methods is judged not in terms of the complex theory which underlies them but in terms of how well they work. Both the new and the old practices appear to be effective in their own ways; both provide their own satisfactions. The government mobile health unit, which has visited Goaso biweekly for several years, and the new, permanent medical dispensary, staffed by trained Ashanti technicians, are besieged by patients seeking scientific help. Many of them doubt somewhat the efficacy of the old supernatural system, but few are willing to place themselves entirely in the hands of the strange new system. And so they make use of both.

The traditional medico-religious specialist does not seem to mind in the least. His prescription for the treatment of a nagging sore throat might well read: give greater respect to your elders, wear this charm around your neck, and ask the medical technician for a shot of penicillin. The fee: three eggs.

Those persons fortunate enough to survive the rigors of a rather difficult life survey the period of their old age with serene anticipation. Unless chronic ill-health mars their days, they look forward to the calm years of a reduction in work and economic responsibility and an increase in leisure for enjoying the fruits of a lifetime. Far from burdening the soul with a dread of loneliness and neglect, the approach of old age ushers in the prospect of heightened respect, devoted filial and family care, and still useful service. And if the attentions of the living are not sufficient, the attainment of a long life assures the elderly that they possess the good will of the gods and ancestors who have acknowledged favorably the many prayers for the blessings of health and age.

This period of life begins for women when they can no longer bear children, for men when they are no longer capable of heavy physical exertion. The veins which, it is believed, tie the body together, become weakened by time and the wear of work, and the aged thus deserve a period of quiet enjoyment. But if the body is thought to reflect the growing exhaustion of time, the mind is not. On the contrary, the mind of the aged is believed to have been strengthened abundantly by long experience, and the well-tempered wisdom of their years is reverently sought in affairs of family and community.

Essential to the general happiness of the elderly person is a family of many children and many more grandchildren, and still more great-grandchildren; to have countless progeny is to have countless blessings, boundless respect, and certain security until the end. Without descendants, these last years of life may well be sad and lonely. Loyal, closely knit families, both matrilineal and patrilineal, serve as an incomparable form of social security, for they provide not only physical care but also the assurance of protection and of a perpetually positive role to be played to the end of life.

But there must be a family. It is in large part for this reason that so great an emphasis is placed upon the bearing of children. The barren woman and the childless man face not only the ridicule of the fertile during their productive years but also the unhappy prospects of a solitary, precarious life when they are old and a melancholy, meager funeral when they die. Each man and woman wants a family, each needs a family.

The ideal old person is one who is financially independent, who is able to contribute of his own resources to the expenses of the household; he should be in fair health, clear in mind, with sparkling wit and engaging conversation. As a storyteller and relater of traditions and wisdom, he is respected and loved by all. As the babies are born to his sons, they may receive his name. As they are born into his lineage, he may be invited to bless them with the good wishes of the ancestors, for, having grown closer to the departed with the passing of the years, he now more clearly knows their intentions and speaks for them. As he plays with his children's children or tends them in the absence of their parents—there is no baby-sitting problem in Ashanti—he knows they will mourn for him at his funeral. They may chide him about his enfeeblement or joke about his approaching demise, but he knows they do so in jest and he lashes back playfully at their seeming lack of respect. Children were not so ill-mannered when he was young, he says, though he knows differently.

Besides, his pride is not vulnerable in the areas of old age and death; he enjoys the one and contemplates the other with only a minimum of anxiety. He never pretends to be younger than he is, and he knows that when he dies these prattling grandchildren will be present to sing stirring memorial odes to his character and achievements and to introduce him to the ancestors with a lavish funeral. Meanwhile, when they need comfort or counsel they come to him, for he has stored up unfathomable amounts of both and it is his place in the family to dispense them generously.

But Ashanti is changing, and with the changes there comes a new, disturbing attitude toward old age. Fewer and fewer old people attain the ideal of life during this period, although the measure of their enjoyment is still considerable. The grounds for their former, respected authority are being undermined. The increasingly complex demands of the new way of life places high premiums upon literacy, upon formal education and new skills which few elderly people have had the opportunity to acquire. The increased dependence upon wealth in money, the growing feeling that the inheritance, as opposed to the achievement, of social rank is outmoded, the insidious suspicion that the ancestors may be less potent than they are supposed to be, the rise of political parties led by young men who argue a different kind of politics, the departure of family members for distant parts, the abandonment of old traditions—all these and other factors contribute to a weakening of the position of the aged in Ashanti. The jokes of children have more sting, the fruits of life are more bitter to the taste. It is with some pain that the old person comes to realize that his accumulated wisdom is frequently ignored, that family and community leadership more and more falls upon those vigorous youths who have been to school, who can read and write and argue with literate men. But he can only accede. He is wise enough to acknowledge some wisdom in the changes and to realize that he could not reverse the trends if he would.

For all this, there is as yet no need to weep for the aged in Ashanti. They enjoy an improved standard of living, they themselves control substantially more wealth than ever before, and, for the most part, their families remain with them. Their position, though weakened, has by no means completely deteriorated. The attitudes toward them fostered by the traditions of hundreds of years and still supported in the main by the institutions of Ashanti society earn them the considerable respect of those younger than they. Most old people can look forward with equanimity to that climax of the good life, a serene old age, a death befitting an Ashanti, and a triumphal journey to the land of the revered ancestors.

The intricate network of social relationships in a well-organized, tightly knit society, in which the interdependence of persons and the prerogatives of rank are important, is seldom better revealed than on the occasion of a funeral. The stranger in Goaso, but recently arrived, without a family and with few friends, is buried unceremoniously at the begrudging expense of the chief and the community Council of Elders. His coffin is of rude planks, hastily nailed together, and his funeral procession consists of a few loafers rounded up to serve as pallbearers, a representative of the chief, and perhaps a straggler or two. He is dead, and the poverty of his interment dramatically emphasizes the warning of parents to children that it is not good to die away from the family and the village which is home.

To die at home after a respected life, however, is to reap a funeral celebration at which the affections and obligations of his own family, or his father's family, of the wife or husband's family and of all others bound to him through ties of marriage, kinship, association, or friendship are generously demonstrated. On the sad day of the death, word is carried quickly or telephoned to other communities summoning the friends and relatives to pay homage to the departed. Throughout the night they gather in the home to sing and testify that an honorable man is coming to be with his ancestors, the dirge-like Christian hymns with verses from the Psalms of David alternating with the death songs of the Ashanti. With low cries of sorrow, the family members bathe the body and place it tenderly in its final bed, a polished mahogany coffin with glass side windows, dressed in its best cloth and resting upon fine blankets. When the next day has come the mourners accompany the coffin to the cemetery—after a Christian funeral service at the church, if the deceased is a Christian—and it is lowered into the grave to be covered with the red earth of Ashanti.

For a week the mourning and fasting continue, until on the seventh day after death the second celebration is held. From all sides, wearing the colors of mourning—the earth colors, orange, deep red, blue, brown, or black—come those who wish to comfort the bereaved and to demonstrate their unity with the deceased and his family in this crisis. But this celebration takes on the flavor of a party, a farewell party, for that, indeed, is what it is. The soul of the dead has begun its journey to the land of departed souls, and this is an event which calls for music, for drumming, for drinking, for dancing and visiting. The gaiety is not unrestrained, because, after all, death does sever intimate personal relationships of long standing, and, while death need not always be feared, it is disquieting and sobering. The pleasure of the social event, this farewell party, is tempered, then, with a sense of solemnity, but not so much as to cast a pall over the proceedings.

The soul's journey, for one thing, is not a very long one; the ancestors are always nearby, and he but joins them. Though he will no longer be visible to men, his presence will still be felt, a very real threat to those who ignore him through social misbehavior, a very real help to those who show their respect for him through social conformity.

He is, furthermore, about to assume a social rank among these ancestors, and one of the best clues to his placement in the society of ancestors is the size and quality of the farewell party tendered him by his mortal friends and family. A niggardly funeral testifies to a niggardly man, a glorious funeral to a beloved father, uncle, and grandfather, a respected leader and friend, and such a man will be given a status among the ancestors commensurate with the demonstrations of affection and obligation presented him by his survivors at the funeral.

So the tears are few and the enjoyment plentiful as the palm wine, gin, and beer flow and the drums rumble and thump their accompaniment for the dances. On through the day runs the celebration, and into the night.

The expression of these interindividual and interfamily ties includes not only attendance at the grand farewell but also a contribution of money to the family for the ostensible purpose of defraying the expenses of the party. This is a realistic approach to a pecuniary problem which could be a sizable hardship to a family in an economy which, while fairly well-to-do for the nonindustrialized world, is not overflowing with money. More than that, the donation of money is a measure of the relationships between the individuals and groups in this society, for the determination of the amount to be contributed depends upon numerous complicated considerations reflecting all the subtle facets of the human ties involved. Among these are the quality of the relationship between the donor and the deceased, the quality of the relationships between their families, the prestige of the deceased and of his family in the community, and the prestige of the donor and his family in the community. All these and other considerations are delicately balanced by a people adept at the delicate balancing of social obligations.

To ensure the public awareness of the donors' evaluations of all these factors, an accounting is made of each gift. The name of each donor and the amount of his donation are recorded by a secretary, and a messenger periodically circulates through the crowd announcing the size and the source of each contribution. Thus the Ashanti not only distribute the burden of the funeral expenses but also encourage the virtue of generosity by a device which, to the unfamiliar, might suggest a rather cynical appraisal of human nature. It is not especially cynical, for the purpose of the loud declaration is not primarily to embarrass potentially niggardly donors or to increase the size of their gifts—although admittedly this may be one of the practical and desirable by-products. The Ashanti regard a virtue as no less virtuous if it is widely recognized and acclaimed, and so when a person fulfills his reciprocal obligations, let it be known. "Kofi Ampofu gives ten shillings!" "Yo, that is good. We shall remember it."

With the music of farewell ringing in his ears, the soul takes his departure on the seventh day after death. On the fortieth day after death a smaller celebration will commemorate another milestone on his journey, and finally, one year after death, the extended family will meet to remember him and to acknowledge his arrival in the land of his ancestors. On Christmas and on New Year's Day, at Easter and on other occasions when public or private ceremonies are held, he will be remembered with mingled sadness and joy. As the generations pass, he fades more and more as a distinct personality until at last he is only one of the general company of the ancestors, whose venerated numbers stretch back to the beginning of Ashanti.

7. Democracy, Old and New

The extended family has been described as essentially a group of relatives living in a single or in neighboring communities under the leadership of the elder men of the family, one of whom is popularly acknowledged as its "head." In some of the simpler of the world's varied societies, politics involves the people in groupings no more complex than this. But this is a far cry from politics in Ashanti. Ashanti lies in a part of the world, West Africa, where several societies had developed forms of government of greater complexity than those of most other areas outside the literate world.

When the British arrived in Kumasi, the capital of Ashanti, in force powerful enough to annex the territory as a colony of the empire, this nation itself constituted a potential empire, strong enough to have carried a war of expansion down to the very guns of British forts in the coastal region of the Gold Coast, as it was then called. This took place less than a century ago and, while Ashanti is now only a constituent part of a larger nation, Ghana, rather than its imperial ruler, not all of its ancient glory has been dissipated. Ashanti's tenure as a British colony was brief—little more than fifty years—and its remembrance of greatness has not died. Its glory may, in fact, have been enhanced during these intervening years, for now Ashanti has acquired a new status in a world which, for the most part, had never heard of it. The British, who came to conquer, have departed with an equal partner in their Commonwealth of Nations, and the name of Ashanti is spoken in places unforeseen even by the ancestors and the gods.

Ashanti's new status is not due solely to its earlier role in West Africa. For one thing, the British have succeeded quite well—whether or not this was their expressed intention—in creating some sense of unity between Ashanti and most of its former enemies or competitors in Ghana; for another, the British have built a foundation of political, economic, and other social skills necessary for participation in world affairs. But the contribution of Ashanti itself to its modern statehood should not be underestimated, for two centuries of experience with complex government have helped to prepare it for the return to self-government which Ghana now enjoys. It is not returning to the past; it is too late for that. But the past is not dead.

In pre-British Ashanti every man and woman had a voice in political affairs. As in a Western democracy, the individual's voice was muted, and the relatively powerless individual found himself paying taxes, going to war, and getting pushed around by individuals and groups with power. But that is a state of affairs impossible to avoid in any political system. It is one of the strengths of democracy that it does permit a number of these comparatively puny individuals to join their voices and say something loud enough to influence the actions of those who do have power. The Ashanti individual had that, above all, in his extended family.

He selected, first of all, the leader of his own extended

family, a position of honor and some authority usually held by an elderly man who had demonstrated qualities of leadership. He himself, as an adult male, also was eligible for election to this post, although deference to the accumulated wisdom of age generally forced postponement of his election until later years. Even a woman could succeed to the headship of a family if she possessed a personality forceful enough to dominate a family of unassertive males; this did not happen often, but it was quite possible. Once acknowledged head of a family, a man's tenure was secure for life, if he maintained only normal amounts of health, sanity, and discretion. If he failed to please his family members by his actions, however, out he went, to be replaced by another more competent and agreeable. Never allowed to become an autocrat, he was essentially a respected, often revered leader, but a leader who required the consent of the led.

Among the major duties of the family head was that of representing his family in community affairs. To do this, he held membership in the Council of Elders, a governing board composed of the heads of all the extended families residing permanently in the community. With one exception, all the elders carried approximately equal power on the council, although the superior numerical strength or wealth or the longer or more noble tradition of one extended family could add weight to its representative's arguments. Influence could be enhanced also by the nature of the family's particular office in the council or by the maintenance of a permanent residence in the capital city, where the higher levels of government were located and where influence could be exerted on more powerful politicians.

The one member of the council whose inherent power slightly exceeded that of any other single member was the headman of the community. His person and office maintained unity in the council and prevented it from degenerating into an arena for factional feuding. He represented that extended family which historically had come to be known as royal, from whose ranks the community headman was always selected; ordinarily, he was also the head of that royal family. His election to the post of headman required the approval of all the members of the Council of Elders. Thus he and his office were subject to several potent democratic controls. He was made eligible for office by his accidental but fortunate birth into the royal family, but his ultimate selection to community headship depended upon the clear recognition of his acquired abilities to lead by three powerful groups: first, by the members of his own family, then by the council representatives of all the other families in the community, and finally, and most democratically, by the individual members of all the families, who registered approval or disapproval through their own representatives. His tenure, like that of any family head, depended upon his behavior. If he failed to please, out he went, to be replaced by another member of the royal family who could gain the necessary approval.

This same pattern of organization existed in various territorial units larger than the community. The headmen of various communities comprising a subdistrict represented their communities on a Council of Elders under the leadership of a subchief who came from the royal lineage of the subdistrict. The subchief of a subdistrict similarly represented his area on a District Council of Elders, made up of the several subchiefs. The district chief, with others like himself, served under a paramount chief of a state, and the paramount chiefs constituted the Ashanti Confederacy Council under the leadership of the most esteemed person in Ashanti, the Asantehene, who himself was the paramount chief of his own state, Kumasi. The individual, commoner or royalty, participated in a series of widening political groupings, each embracing successively larger territories, populations, and kin groups in a bureaucratic, hierarchical structure, balanced on each level by the wants of the individual Ashanti citizen and possessing a large measure of decentralized power and authority.

This outline of the political structure really does not do justice to its complexity. Not all chiefs, for example, served simultaneously on two levels of government; when they did not, other representatives were selected to do so. Not all subordinates enjoyed equal access to their superiors in the bureaucracy; if they did not, intermediaries served as liaison officers between them, thus further increasing the number of politicians to be kept in style. In addition, there was a distaff side to politics. Usually in the background of what was primarily the manly pursuit of government stood a woman, the queen mother, a close matrilineal relative of the head chief and a bona fide member of the Council of Elders. Frequently saying but little in public or conveying her opinions in whispers or laying down the law to the chief before and after conferences, she was a power to reckon with, particularly when the time came to select personnel for government posts.

For all the politicians there was a host of aides and consultants and spokesmen and intermediaries, all considered necessary to the gathering of information, the making of decisions, the behind-the-scenes arranging of deals, and the observance of an elaborate political etiquette and protocol. Among these was the spokesman, whose elaborately carved, gold-leafed stave symbolized his office. Persons addressing the chief did so through him, and through him, in turn, the chief replied, for the respect in which the chief was held placed him above direct argument or even discussion with his inferiors.

In addition there were the collectors of internal revenue. Financing a political superstructure like that of Ashanti was no mean task, and these resourceful people had successfully explored many of the avenues for getting revenue known to modern governments. Among the familiar or unfamiliar devices employed were inheritance taxes on personal property— these were not, however, levied on land—taxes on the income from mining, farming, hunting, and fishing; government monopolies on certain types of trade; court fines and fees; special levies for war and for the installation of new chiefs; and levies on war booty and on funerals. All in all, this is an impressive list which does credit to the imagination of bureaucrats devoted to maintaining an orderly government worthy of a wealthy nation, to expanding the empire, and to supporting themselves in the manner to which they had, through the years, become accustomed. Goaso paid its share of the costs—not always willingly—in exchange for good government. They paid more, too, in life and blood and sorrow as citizens and soldiers in the armies of Ashanti. But they usually got good government.

Early in the eighteenth century a number of states in the central part of Ashanti, in and around Kumasi, the present capital, voluntarily merged in a confederacy. For unknown centuries these states had shared a common language and culture but had persisted in maintaining separate political establishments in adjacent territories. Then several events occurred which drastically altered the politics of an era. There was probably an increase in population that forced expansion into lightly inhabited territories. More important, the rise of the slave trade with Europeans, who shipped millions of slaves to the sugar and cotton plantations of the New World, brought increased wealth and those persuasive tools of empire, guns and ammunition, into the hands of the Ashanti. These people were primarily wholesalers and retailers of war and slave captives, although considerable numbers of the Ashanti themselves were trapped and sold into the stinking holds to be hauled to the Americas. It was in this era of prosperity and growing power that a brilliant Ashanti priest and a succession of aggressive chiefs emerged to add a new political concept to the old fusion of religion and politics. This new concept was a confederation of states, sanctioned in part by a miraculous religious revelation, which they succeeded in realizing about A.D. 1700.

By treaty or by conquest, more and more neighboring states were incorporated into the Confederacy, and the expansion continued slowly but steadily up to the time that England, Germany, and France made the fateful decision to increase and consolidate their West African holdings in the second half of the nineteenth century. As the Confederacy mushroomed during the eighteenth and nineteenth centuries, the eventual fifteen member states were permitted to retain considerable autonomy, though each was required to subordinate its own interests to the Confederacy Council and the Asantehene when the common welfare demanded it. On an elaborate scale, the essential features of restricted governing authority in the extended family and in the community were retained on the confederacy level. The maintenance of effective checks and balances upon the power of any individual, any small clique, or any large state was of paramount interest to each of the member states, and smart political management borrowed the traditional family restraints and built them solidly into the confederacy organization.

At the top of the hierarchy, the Asantehene ruled with a council in which his authority was just slightly superior to that of each of its members. He, like them, was born to a royal clan, but he was also subject to the citizens both of the state which selected him and of the entire Confederacy. If he failed to please them, he was deposed, to be replaced by someone else from his royal clan who could conduct affairs properly. The amount of organization and drive necessary to work a change of personnel at the top was considerable, to be sure, for at this level the chiefs held great power and prestige and, usually, ability. But the mechanisms of control were present, and on occasion they were put to effective use by aspiring men who could campaign subtly and make deals shrewdly to oust officeholders and replace them with themselves. And through it all the small voice of the individual could be heard in the affairs of state. Few governments can do better by their citizens.

Goaso and the Ahafo District, of which it is a part, have never been in the foreground of Ashanti or Ghana politics because of their distance from the centers of population and activity and because of their pattern of settlement. Goaso's ancestors, citizens of one of the more important independent states, Denkyera, not far from Kumasi in the year 1700, had made a grievous miscalculation of the Confederacy's strength and had chosen to fight it rather than to join it. After a military victory which assured the future of the Confederacy, the defeated survivors either fled to the southwest or were taken prisoner and enslaved. The fate of the latter was not uniformly bad, for the majority of them were "adopted" into Ashanti society and eventually resettled in the western districts of the Confederacy. The Ahafo District, owned and controlled largely by members of the Kumasi state bureaucracy, is one such settlement center. Here, the stigma of their ignoble origin largely though not completely dissipated, the people of Goaso and of the neighboring communities have had to limit their political activities primarily to local and district affairs. Their form of government, however, is identical with that throughout the rest of the Confederacy, and their representatives speak for them in Kumasi—not always well, for, on the higher levels of the Ashanti Confederacy, Goaso's "owners" and principal representatives are descended from Kumasi conquerors, Goaso's people only from the conquered.

The essential traditional balance between the member states and the nation, between districts and the state, between communities and districts, between royalty and commoner, between the governing and the governed has been upset by British colonial policy during the past fifty or sixty years. Disruption of the old patterns was inevitable, despite British attempts to minimize it by imposing political controls as much as possible like the traditional system. Calling their system of government "Indirect Rule," the British have tried to support the chiefs in positions of relatively high status and authority by permitting them to keep some of their old chiefly prerogatives while at the same time using them as spokesmen and agents for the new powers of the British central government. The scheme has had some success, although the success has not taken exactly the form expected. For, while the chiefs are still chiefs in Ashanti, the British are no longer rulers, a development they had pledged themselves to effect but without serious expectation of such rapid achievement. The political changes initiated by the British have proceeded at such a vigorous pace that, after only sixty years, the colonial officers have packed their official bags, although some may remain as employees of the new government to conduct, in either advisory or authoritative capacities, many of the functions they formerly performed as civil servants of the crown.

The chiefs, however, have not been able completely to maintain their old positions, a deterioration reflected in recent years by an epidemic of short-tenured chiefs at all levels except at the very top. It is not difficult to see why this has happened. For one thing, to the traditional qualifications for political office, royal birth, sanity, sobriety, good health, wisdom—usually achieved with age and experience—eloquence, and generosity, have been added those of literacy, a desire to build roads and schools and to promote social welfare programs, and the ability to represent the people adequately before the British government officers.

The chief has had to satisfy not only his constituents but also the British, who reserved the right to demand replacement of the incompetent or the unco-operative—by British standards, however tolerant these might have been. As if this were not threat enough to chiefs, who have always preferred to die quietly of old age while still in office, everyone has realized that they have held their posts just so long as the foreign rulers have smiled upon them. The chief who has held office at the sufferance of the British has had difficulty getting his people to kneel humbly before him and reverently to call him "grandfather." The servant-citizen who has sworn allegiance today might next week himself be chief, a possibility which contributes little to the chiefly peace of mind. It has taken a shrewd man, indeed, to be a chief, to appease all factions, to belong to no party and to belong to all parties simultaneously, and only the most shrewd have survived in office long enough to be buried in state.

The Ashanti political system requires that its leaders earn and keep the approval of the governed, and when the prescribed, controlled means for doing so are pulled out from under the throne it topples. In this society, where politics has traditionally been an exciting game, a number of people have always been jockeying for power; traffic to and from, on and off chiefly thrones—never a light traffic—increased tremendously under British rule. Even rural, relatively quiet, inconspicuous Goaso had five headmen between 1920 and 1937, only one of whom died in office. The others succumbed before charges of drunkenness, witchcraft, and general incompetence. The present headman has survived seventeen years of successful if unspectacular administration, but survival in office is itself a spectacular achievement for any politician these days. He has been fortunate, however, to occupy a post of relatively minor importance, or he would long since have entered the political limbo reserved for deposed chiefs.

He is, in many respects, in an unenviable position. Not only are there likely to be people within his own extended family and even outside his family who cast covetous glances at his office, but the headman of Goaso has been pushed and prodded by the "Native Authority," that long arm of the British Colonial Office which reached out to manage or influence most affairs even in his small domain. Its officials intercepted the revenue which once had entered his pocket—and, significantly, left almost as quickly, part of it to be returned in services and payment of obligations to the citizens, part of it to enter pockets higher up in the bureaucracy, part of it to maintain his own somewhat higher standard of living. Under the British the government handled most receipts and disbursements. The Native Authority ordered him to develop his town and area. It rewrote much of the traditional

Ashanti civil and criminal codes. He has been a headman or a chief, but sadly diminished in power.

But he has been more than a canopied figurehead. The government has allowed him to exercise his traditional jurisdiction over the land, a most enlightened allowance, he feels, because it has permitted his people to win their wealth from land which they themselves continue to own. Because of the Western craving for chocolate, ownership of their own cocoa farms has made Ashanti farmers wealthier than most of their colonial counterparts in the rest of the world. The chief of Goaso happily sits near this source of income; he has a box seat with an excellent view of the proceedings.

He does continue to serve as an arbitrator, sometimes as a judge, in interfamily disputes. He intercedes on behalf of his people before the ancestors in religious ceremonies and he represents the moral force of the ancestors as they criticize or applaud the actions of their children. As a judge in an officially recognized, though low-level, court he can hear civil cases in which damages do not exceed $140, suits for divorce in non-Christian marriages, suits relating to the inheritance of property valued at not more than $560, or criminal cases in which the fine is not more than $70 or the imprisonment not more than three months.

These rights are something, but they are not much. Even as judge in so minor a court he has been constantly reminded that the basic sanction for his office has resided in the British government, for sitting in the court with him and his chief-colleagues there has also been a clerk, the registrar of the Native Authority, a paid African employee of the government, usually a commoner, frequently not even an Ashanti. Because the registrar has necessarily been literate and hired and trained by the British, he has been empowered to act as prosecutor, counsel for the defense, clerk of the court, court stenographer, and on occasion even the interpreter of the new law to the judges. When an Ashanti chief needs an interpreter of the law, particularly in the person of some commoner from out-of-the-state, perhaps even from outside Ashanti, he is but a shadow of his ancestors.

His financial rewards have shrunk in proportion to his political stature. The salary paid him by the government he regards as little more than a pittance. In many communities like Goaso, the headmen are hardly distinguishable from the commoners, for on Monday morning they and their families are likely to be found hard at work on their farms. His income has become largely what he can earn by farming or can acquire through the performance of his customary, ritual duties or can pick up discreetly from the performance of some sub-customary, sub rosa duties. The latter resource presents an uncertain amount of danger, however, for there have been continually on the scene clerks and auditors with sharp eyes, excellent at accounting, experienced in the ways of the world, and with disrespectful souls devoid of mercy—or usually so.

For all this, he has kept some substance of his former self. The status of headman and chief is still such as to keep him in wary competition with those who connive to overthrow him. Ashanti's past is still sufficiently present to offer prestige to the man who holds this position. It is a degree of prestige, furthermore, not yet completely available to commoners in a society where only royal ancestry and royal office could traditionally confer honor, power, and wealth. The headman of Goaso, wearing the noble symbols of his office—the armlets and crown of carved wood leafed with gold—and sheltered as a chief should be by a royal canopy held by servants, is proud of his office and would not willingly forsake it. Nor

The road to Goaso winds through a tropical rain forest and brings the traveler to the town's main street.

The Ashanti girl, on reaching puberty, is the center of a week of festivities honoring her newly acquired status as a woman. Both the women and the girls leave the fields early in the afternoon to bring home food and firewood and start preparing the evening meal for the head of the family.

For generations, the Goa River has supplied water for drinking, cooking, and bathing, as well as for doing the laundry. Some of the children have gathered to swim in a nearby pool. The girl at the left combines business with pleasure as she sells peanuts from her tray.

The plaited hair of the priest of the god Bonsam distinguishes him from the other men who wear their hair cropped short. For eight days in a nine day cycle, he is a cocoa farmer like his neighbors.

On the ninth day he becomes the incarnation of the god, and while thus possessed he presides at ceremonies in which the petitions of his people are received and evidence of his concern for them is given.

New homes in Goaso are built by lashing together vertical and horizontal poles and filling the spaces with mud. An example of the finished product can be seen in the background, behind the Christian funeral procession. In the procession are children from one of the two schools in Goaso, both of which are operated by the mission churches.

The golden pods of cocoa are cut down, the brown beans extracted and stored in a warehouse. The government's marketing board protects the farmer by stabilizing prices and storing any surplus of the one cash crop of the Ashanti farmer.

As a symbol of his office, the spokesman for the chief carries a beautifully carved stave, covered with gold leaf. Anyone who addresses the chief must do so through the spokesman.

would the queen mother yield her honorable post without a struggle. Usually a wise, elderly woman from the royal family, the queen mother represents the interests of all the women of the town in political issues brought before the Council of Elders, of which she is a quiet but potent member.

There is still more to this chiefship than the frustrations the chief's restricted authority suggest. He is more than a mayor. Indeed, he is more than a governor or president, for he is motivated in part by religious considerations which are stronger than the call to political duty of civic-mindedness, national patriotism, lordly power, or easy money. As headman, or chief, he is the current representative of the generations of venerable ancestors who have held this office before him. Because the ancestors inhabit both their invisible world and the present, visible, human world, he stands as the duly selected intermediary between them and the society which they created and over which they in a real sense preside. The land and the families over which he appears to preside are simply in his keeping, and he is obligated to fulfill the exacting terms of his trusteeship.

More mundane considerations also motivate him, to be sure. To be addressed as "grandfather" by grown men who kneel before him with shoulder bared and sandals removed, is flattering; to receive the deference of government officers is soothing; to sit in judgment is ego strengthening; to collect the emoluments of office is reassuring; to outwit competitors is exciting. But all these gratifications also please the ancestors, and to please them is one of the highest values of this life. He is bound and supported, then, by an unwritten constitution of men, visible and invisible, and of law, derived from the experience of past centuries. His rights and obligations extend to those mortals entrusted to his care and to

117

those immortals whose memory and way of life he is pledged to preserve. His is an honorable office, even a crucial one, and—this may eventually prove to be most important—its position in the new Ghana government is not yet finally determined. It is not impossible that Ashanti chiefs may regain a degree of authority comparable to that which their ancestors once enjoyed.

Caught between the high ideals of a romanticized past and the disconcerting pressures of modern times, headmen and chiefs find the present going rough. Even staying in office exacts its toll. For four or five years Goaso's headman has been suffering from "stomach pains," and a succession of visits to the hospital and to traditional physicians has failed to bring relief. He does not know the diagnosis, but any Western businessman could make a plausible guess. Whatever the trouble may be, neither European medicines nor Ashanti charms or prayers seem to be helping much. There is a good chance that he would feel better if he got out of politics and drank plenty of milk. But there is discouragingly little milk in Goaso, and successful politicking has its own high rewards even in Goaso.

In local government, of which the Native Authority has been a part, the British placed increased reliance upon commoners who proved themselves capable of taking responsibilities as the British defined them. This was not a completely strange role for commoners, for the democratic bases of Ashanti life were established long before the arrival of European democracy. So vigorously have commoners exploited their new opportunity for, at the very least, near equality with royalty, that they have tended in the past decade to overshadow in importance and power the lesser chiefs and headmen. Nowhere is this more dramatically observed than on the level of national Ghana politics, where men and even a woman with little or no claim to royalty campaign for elective offices, making free use of invective and ward heelers in the best Western, un-Ashanti political tradition. And such candidates are elected, the ancestors notwithstanding. Similarly, in local districts, the weight of government falls more and more upon those who can prove their qualifications on grounds other than those of royal birth and inherited authority, on such rational grounds as modern competence or on the emotional grounds of personal persuasiveness or charm.

Once upon a time, each member of the Council of Elders had a special function, one of them serving as a commander in chief, three serving as commanders of the three army divisions, one serving as overseer of the royal household, another as superintendent of the royal bodyguard, another as spokesman for the chief. Now, however, with warfare at an end and the national police in control, few members of the council have any specifically differentiated services to perform. They may retain their ceremonial titles and may reminisce nostalgically about their predecessors in the days before Ashanti was spoiled by the invaders, but their major administrative functions are carried out by the new bureaucrats, British and African, bright young men in business suits or khaki dress evaluating reports in central offices equipped with typewriters and other business machines.

The annual budget meeting in Goaso, headquarters for the Ahafo District held in a recent year prior to independence, provides a clear, summary look into the administration of a modern, colonial, rural area on the verge—some European pessimists would use "brink"—of self-government. There is more, much more, to colonial administration than can emerge from a budget meeting in Goaso, but such an assembly does show what has been happening at the colonial grass roots in much of rural Africa, which is where the majority of people live.

The meeting was called by the British government officer. It was open to all who cared to attend in addition to the Area Committee, composed of Africans, all of them commoners of some distinction, and the community headmen and chiefs. Presented for general approval was a program of services and development for the ensuing year. A statement of receipts and disbursements demonstrated to the people what they had paid for and received from their modern government. They learned that nearly 60 per cent of the district revenue came from the ordinary taxes and levies placed upon them either by the national government, principally through a head tax, or voluntarily by themselves. About 40 per cent of their district income consisted of a subsidy from the Gold Coast government, the amount of which was dependent upon the taxes and levies collected in the district during the previous fiscal year.

During that year the administration of the Ahafo District, with a population of about 25,000, received a total of roughly $60,000 with which to conduct its business. This sum was disbursed for such services as administrative and treasury costs, native court and police costs, medical services, education and social welfare services, roads and communication services, and a few miscellaneous items. "Extraordinary expenditures" went toward the building of a maternity clinic, an area office building, a new road, reservoirs for several community water supplies, market construction, and the building of incinerators for refuse disposal in several communities. A surplus of about $600 was allocated to a scholarship fund for Ahafo District students.

Most of these items were approved without discussion, although impassioned argument, a good deal of it irrelevant, flared on the issue of wage scales for schoolteachers. Too low, too low to induce young people into this crucial profession was the verdict—though, of course, argument was to no immediate avail, since the umpires were located out of earshot in the faraway offices of the government Department of Education. The meager amount dedicated to scholarships also was criticized, and perhaps the majority would have diverted the office building fund into the scholarship fund—an argument also without effect, because, as the British officer pointed out, the district must house its operations in an edifice worthy of orderly, democratic government. For a few minutes, too, the meeting threatened to become an arena in which the young gladiators from two neighboring towns, squabbling over the boundaries to the rich cocoa lands lying between them, were willing to settle then and there the dispute which was being fought in the Ashanti courts in an orderly and legal but far more expensive manner. Reason prevailed.

It was not a quiet affair. The high value placed by the Ashanti upon rhetoric and litigation was clearly reflected—reflected frequently and simultaneously by five or six hoarse, masculine voices, none of them in unison. Contributing to the din was a certain amount of confusion over whom to address at the meeting. The "presiding" Ahafo chiefs, three of them, were seated upon a raised platform at the front of the assembly, in deference to their august personages; the two British "advisers" occupied ground-floor seats, separated from the other participants, as befitted alien and powerful, if devoted and benign, intruders. This made it possible for the assembled to carry on a minimum of two arguments simultaneously, and they did. Final decisions came from the two seats on the ground floor.

Still, this was a democratic process. The meeting achieved its purpose with a smoothness—and hardly a threat of fisticuffs—which revealed the quality of planning and organization that had preceded it. Area Committee members and chiefs had had the opportunity to evaluate and amend basic decisions during conferences held prior to the budget's public presentation, and even at the budget meeting minor revisions suggested from the floor were allowed. If the budget meeting did not conclusively demonstrate the capabilities of rural districts to run their own affairs in the immediate future, it did show that, even without the British, African leadership trained in local government administration stands a good chance of building a new, modern, effective democracy on older, traditional, democratic foundations.

Among the institutions employed in rural communities for civic improvement is that of the voluntary communal work party, a modern version of a community service organization found throughout Ashanti for centuries. Every week or two the call is sent out by the chief to all able-bodied young adult men to donate a day or two of free labor to the common welfare. Their work consists of digging a drainage ditch in Goaso's main street, digging a public latrine beyond the outskirts of town, cutting and burning the rapidly growing bush which forever threatens to entangle the town or to infest it with the pests it harbors, adding a room to one of the schools, repairing one of the churches, or any one of numerous other projects which a progressive community continually promotes.

It is not unusual to see three or four young men at work while others offer encouragement and sound advice. After

all, there are plenty of reasons for not working too strenu-
ously; the heat, intestinal troubles, and a feeling that Goaso
will be here for quite a while, that Goaso formerly got along
without a drainage ditch, and that the ditch can be completed
just as well next week. Besides, this ditchdigging is a labor of
love, an occasion to be enjoyed as much as possible.

The Ashanti political scene is one of change, of revision
and uncertainty, of tension between old and new statuses,
between old and new modes of life. The factors producing
these shifts in behavior and viewpoints are complex, but one
of them—the school—stands out and deserves attention. The
development of the school is, of course, dependent upon other
factors, but they can be ignored for the moment, so that
the role of the school in modern Ashanti can itself be explored. The school not only reflects the changes which are
occurring but also, as one of the major means by which an
Ashanti child becomes a part of his modern Ashanti society,
reinforces those changes and speeds the pace at which they
occur. These effects may be summarized in a consideration of
two kinds of change.

The first is the remarkable, though hardly surprising,
change being wrought in the manner of bestowing prestige in
Ashanti society. Pre-British Ashanti recognized roughly three
classes of society: royalty, free commoner, and slave. Each
political level, from local community to the Confederacy, had
its own royal extended family, lineage, or clan. These did not
necessarily coincide; Goaso, for example, recognized its local
royalty in an extended family which was not royal on the
Confederacy level, and Goaso elected its headmen, therefore,
from an extended family whose members were never eligible
for the throne of the Asantehene. In Goaso members of the

royal clan of Ashanti, from which the Asantehene was chosen, were ineligible for the headship. This arrangement, probably originating at a time when only one or two families or lineages inhabited a community, made for a balance of power between clans throughout the Confederacy at a later time when greater mobility resulted in numerous families or lineages inhabiting the same area. In any community or district, however, that family, lineage, or clan which was acknowledged as royal held the greatest prestige, and its members enjoyed a superior rank simply by virtue of their fortunate birth to a royal woman. Free commoners had the medium fortune of being born to free common mothers, slaves the misfortune of having a slave mother. Slave women were often adopted into a free common or even into a royal family in order to replenish its numbers, and their children occupied a kind of in-between status, theoretically and sometimes actually free but with a slight slave stigma nonetheless.

Membership in these classes was semirigidly fixed. Marriage between them was permitted—members of the royal family, as of any family, had to marry outside their clan to avoid breaking the incest rules—but marriage to royalty did not confer royalty upon a woman or her children. This was a line which could not be crossed, and only by revolution could a free commoner acquire the political prerogatives and the prestige which the royal-born automatically inherited at birth. Through the generosity of their captors, slaves might acquire the status of free commoner, but the stigma of their origins almost always clung to them, and they generally remained on or near the lowest rung of the "middle-class" prestige ladder.

Today, however, these distinctions are being changed, not so much by the abolition of any class—slavery was legally abolished by the British, though the memory lingers on—as by the adoption of new criteria for determining prestige. Where once birth and growth to adulthood in a royal lineage conferred honor and opportunity, now the acquisition of literacy, education, and greater economic wealth places a man in a strong position to gain prestige and even to manipulate royalty and to challenge the traditional royal claims to political leadership.

Early in the history of schools in Ashanti, the children of slaves rather than the children of the better-born were sent to sit in the hot rooms on the hard benches, to be drilled in the dubious arts of scrawling penciled marks and squinting at printed pages. But this was in the days when the advantages of the new way of life had not yet been recognized. Now even the children of royalty must attend school if they are to have any hope of maintaining their old position: while formal political leadership in many traditional offices still falls to the eligible members of royal lineages, those who are better educated are invariaby chosen over those who are not. Informal political leadership and appointive posts, furthermore, are won by men who are at least literate, and those who run for elective offices on district, state, and national levels do so with little regard to their humble, nonroyal origins. They may almost be said to disregard their origins, a far cry from the time when proper birth meant great opportunity.

A throne-studded genealogy counts for less and less, and the ancestors are no longer thought to be unduly horrified at the turn of events. Ancestors everywhere have a way of adjusting progressively, if at times hesitantly, to changing circumstances. Eventually they even come to think as their descendants do. And an increasing number of people come really not to care what the ancestors think.

There is an almost magical quality to the desire for schooling which is accelerating these changes. It is as if the familiar maxim had been altered to read "in schooling there is power," any schooling, and as much as possible. Even "real" magic is used by parents, pupils, and in some cases, teachers, all of whom want desperately to acquire the power which seems to come with education. The sale of "brain pills" and "rings for learning" has become a fairly lucrative racket—the United States exports both—and séances with powerful priests who guarantee success have increased greatly.

But there are also rational supports for this shift in emphasis upon prestige-through-royal-birth to prestige-through-schooling. It is the literate man who can lift the status of his entire family in the community. It is the literate man who has the wider occupational opportunities and who, presumably, has the greater potentialities for accumulating wealth and the power which more and more it seems to confer. It is the educated man who is now obviously qualified for political posts, as most able to deal with the enormous problems of a district, state, and nation which are growing in complexity. Even in rural Ashanti the relatively small-scale problems of development require the skills of an educated man for their solution. And as for the state and nation, international conferences, constitutional assemblies, fiscal policies, inflation control, economic development programs involving hundreds of millions of dollars, the attraction of foreign investment capital—these are not jobs for men who have nothing to recommend them other than their birth to a royal woman.

Little wonder, then, that a member of Goaso royalty, when

introduced for the first time to an anthropologist who asked permission to live in his town for nearly a year, should respond, "What is there to learn? The price of cocoa has gone up, and our boys are doing well in school." Such a remark from royalty reveals a changing Goaso. The unborn child still does himself a favor by being born to a royal mother, but the really shrewd child also makes sure that he has a father who will send him to school and a mother's brother whose expanding cocoa farms are heavy with the golden pods. If he must choose among these three, the latter two are undoubtedly the course of modern Ashanti wisdom. It was not always so.

The second aspect of social change to be tremendously accelerated, though not solely determined, by the schools is the steady awakening of a national consciousness which is in startling contrast to the old social and regional isolationism. Out of four major, disunited areas, some of them lacking even internal political unity, a relatively united nation, Ghana, is coming into being, and the schools provide an integrative agency of considerable proportions. Through them children and young people throughout the growing nation are acquiring a common body of knowledge, a common awareness of the institutions and potentialities of a world and of fields of learning once unknown, and a common desire to appropriate some of their achievements and values.

Through them, too, children are brought into immediate relationship with those individuals, the teachers, who, in rural areas especially, have had the most effective contact with this new world and who constitute one of the most vocal, restless, and able segments of the society proposing radical changes in the old way of life. Teachers by no means constitute an organized group of agitators or subversives. Many of them are young and poorly educated themselves. Their opinions are often resisted by the more conservative older generation, which regards them as spoiled, callow upstarts—while at the same time envying their skills. But the very nature of their work requires them to teach their eager audiences some of the knowledge and skills which the Western world has brought to Ghana. The result, in this country which is more able than most underdeveloped areas economically to support change, is a simmering political nationalism. Fortunately, it has not boiled over into extreme violence, and the indications are that it will not do so.

Among teachers, and especially among the younger generation of teachers, as among students generally, there is a growing suspicion of the social, economic, political, and religious beliefs of their grandparents. Ancestors, gods, rituals, and the inherent right of royalty to rule—these old truths are questioned. And to question these once solid truths is to doubt them. There is also a particular, passionate dislike for the realities of the colonial system in which they and their parents have lived as subordinates. The inequalities of that system and the rise in the past twenty years of a world opinion which condemns it rather vigorously—and sometimes unrealistically—has inflamed in most Ashanti the desire for a recognized equality, for independent self-government, for free participation in the world. This is not a blanket hatred of colonialism, for, as most of them will admit—some few will admit absolutely nothing— it is the British colonial system as it functioned in Ghana which helped bring them to the point they have now reached, over the threshold of their independence. It is this system, after all, which has built the schools and trained the teachers, has permitted them to keep their rich land and its products, and has gradually taught them the economic, political, and social skills necessary to maintain their freedom in a huge, impersonal world which makes freedom a costly, difficult prize.

But criticism flows like a torrent when the dam of colonialism begins to crumble. In some instances—education, for example, or in the training of Africans for modern political roles—the Ashanti feel that the system has not gone far enough fast enough. In other instances—in the imposition of economic and political controls—they hold that the system has gone too far. The net result is a general and intense, though not for most people absolute or blind, resentment of colonialism. Once open criticism becomes possible, it is the dissatisfactions and frustrations rather than the satisfactions and appreciations that are voiced, and, informally but positively, teachers and students have carried on the campaign inside and outside the classrooms. Most ears have been willing to hear, most tongues to repeat.

So it is that, both through the formal content of the curriculum, which opens new areas of knowledge and freer, imaginative thinking, and through the informal expression of political attitudes, a sense of national unity has been fostered by teachers and schools. These partial products of the Western world have reinforced the opposition to colonialism, have created doubt about old cultural verities, and have spread a new, common culture among previously diverse peoples. This nationalism is not solely an artificial outgrowth of the schools; teachers and students reflect as well as effect events, movements, and attitudes in the whole society. It is not even a completely conscious creation, but teachers and their classrooms are effective agents for strengthening and extending the newer values—and ranking high among these stands Ghana nationalism.

Ghana nationalism does not yet grip the people as it does the peoples of the much-divided Western world. It is too early for that; there are still too many chances for the one nation to remain divisible. There is even a possibility that old political rivalries will arise again or that new ones will emerge to wreck a unity not yet achieved. The Ashanti are still a proud people among proud peoples and, indeed, even at this early date in Ghana national history they are the spearhead of an opposition movement which seeks to decentralize the authority of the national government in favor of greater regional autonomy and greater authority for chiefs. But fifty years ago the very concept of nationalism was alien to the entire region. Then there were Fanti and Nzima and Ga and Accra and Akim-Abuakwa and Akim-Kotoku and Ashanti and Wenchi and Dagomba and Tallensi, and a host of others. Then the term "Ghana" held no meaning for these largely independent Africans. But there were few teachers and fewer schools, few pupils, and little to learn that made sense. Today, however, there are teachers and schools and pupils and much to learn which unites these once divided peoples into a single nation.

8. Money Grows on Trees

A satisfying way of life can develop in economically poor societies, but an elaborate culture like that of both traditional and contemporary Ashanti requires a relatively rich society, a society in which the producers of goods produce enough to feed, clothe, and shelter those who work at politics and religion, those who hire others to do their work, those too young or too old or too ill to work, those who prefer and can afford just to sit around and talk. Ashanti supports all of these, some of them very well indeed. It is the economy which helps make and keep a proud people proud.

Today's business in Goaso is carried on in terms of British pounds, shillings, and pence, but the use of money itself is nothing new to the Ashanti. They, like many West African peoples, had long had a monetary system of their own—using cowrie shells and gold dust as a medium of exchange and as a standard of value—Goaso's market was a miniature of the larger markets to be found in all of Ashanti's cities and towns, and the existence of such a sophisticated, if small-scale, money-price-and-market system for the distribution of goods has undoubtedly helped make possible the rapid, easy transition into the European economic system which is a characteristic of much of West Africa. The extension of credit and taxation also were familiar to the Ashanti and represent nothing essentially new to the culture.

The volume of transactions in modern times involving money or credit, however, far exceeds anything previously encountered, and it is probably fair to say that by now the Ashanti are money-dependent. At the very least, their economy and their whole way of life would suffer a disheartening, even tragic, disruption were a financial crisis to occur within their country or within the sterling or the dollar area. Before the British arrived, a large sector of the economy did not require the exchange of money. For the most part, the very people—members of the extended family—who produced the goods and services for the society also consumed the goods and services they produced. Families and communities were either self-subsistent or nearly so. Exchange of most economic goods occurred within the extended family and required no payment other than reciprocal services or bartered commodities; the same system governed exchange between families or even between communities. Money, therefore, served in those days as a supplement to what was basically a barter system and was used primarily to buy only those goods which could not be obtained through the usual channels. Most Ashanti produced something for cash sale and profit, but few were completely dependent upon money incomes for their livelihood.

Now, however, Goaso's thousand people have become so much a part of the world that their welfare fluctuates directly with the rise and fall of prices in markets far removed from its lanes and fields. Primarily responsible for this dependence upon money and upon international markets is the introduction into the economy of a cash crop, cocoa, and its enthusiastic acceptance by Ghana farmers already familiar with systems of money exchange and production for profit.

Prior to the coming of the Europeans, the emphasis in economic production in Goaso was on subsistence goods, agricultural and animal. Relatively small food surpluses were transported to cities like Kumasi for sale at a profit, but the greatest proportion of produce was consumed by the community and even solely by the family of the producer. Goaso still feeds itself on its own agricultural products, yams, plantains, cocoyams, cassava, and other vegetables and fruits more familiar to American tables. Sheep, goats, chickens, pigs, and small wild game provide the bulk of the meat supply. Beef must be imported on the hoof and slaughtered within a few days, because the tsetse fly carries a disease fatal to cattle and horses and prevents the development of any cattle industry. Many of the food plants now cultivated in Goaso were first domesticated by the American Indians and brought to Africa by the Portuguese and other Europeans, and some of the foods have an untraceable but probable origin in southern Asia. But the techniques of gardening and a sedentary way of life based upon it were known to the Ashanti long before white men came with their new plants.

Supplementing these cultivated crops are the wild-growing natural resources of the forest area, some of which, like the oil palm, are exploited in exhaustive fashion to provide not only food but shelter, heat, light, clothing, medicine, soap, cosmetics, weapons, tools, toys, and above all, on a hot, exhausting day, a soothing, fermented wine—palm wine. Game in the area has become small in size and scarce in quantity. The noise of human society—singing and shouting, toiling and playing, building its houses and working its farms, cutting its roads through the forests and shooting its guns—has in this century almost completely silenced the roar of jungle cats and the thunder of elephants, and frightened away many of the timid, hoofed animals. Even the larger anthropoids are an oddity, although smaller monkeys are still sometimes available for dinner in the late afternoon. Fresh fish from the streams and smoked fish imported from the distant coast—all Goaso and environs can easily detect its odorous arrival by open truck— fill out the meat menu.

Goaso still lives predominantly on what it grows, but the shelves in the stores and market booths contain more and more cans and wrappers which attract Goaso housewives. Condensed milk helps to fill the local lactic void created by the tsetse fly, and canned sardines and corned beef are available everywhere. Soap, matches, kerosene, clothing, cosmetics, liquor, and hardware can all be bought with cash. But most products come from the farms of the family, and sufficient food surpluses are still being raised, although in steadily diminishing quantities, to support a small export trade to the cities.

Ashanti's cities, dependent upon their imports from Goaso and similar rural areas, are facing mounting shortages of food-stuffs as more and more acreage is diverted from the cultivation of food crops to the growing of cocoa for cash. Cocoa has revolutionized the Ashanti economy. Nearly 40 per cent of the world's supply of chocolate and other cocoa products is manufactured from the gold and brown fruit of Ghana's cocoa trees, and Goaso's farmers—nearly everyone in Goaso is a cocoa farmer—pluck their share of the proceeds. Goaso farmers are no more eager to divulge their incomes than are American farmers, workers, or businessmen, but a rough estimate of $600 per year as a mean gross income per producing unit (individual or immediate family) does not appear to be out of line. Many farmers, of course, earn no more than a few hundred dollars, but some few can count their gross receipts up to between $5,000 and $10,000. The female head of one family in a wealthy town near Goaso is rumored to control family lands producing close to $30,000 worth of cocoa annually—which, if true, is rather advanced for a "backward area." The absence of an income tax and the low or non-existent costs of food and shelter have left the Goaso farmer in a better financial position than most people in the world's underdeveloped areas.

Income, furthermore, is widely distributed, for British colonial policy prevented alienation of farm lands to Europeans and maintained the traditional patterns of Ashanti landownership. Here and there mineral rights and timber concessions are in the hands of European enterprise or the national government, but for the most part Ashanti is a land where the small farmer controls his own fields, cultivates and sells his own crops, and enjoys his income as he wishes. Though not all the factors in his livelihood are under his control, he nevertheless has been protected from a foreign-owned and -operated plantation system. If he, as an individual, must answer to his family members for his use of the land, they, at least, are *his* family. No overseas lord gives him food, shelter, and a few shillings a day for his labor. He is his own lord—within the limits allowed by his family and its position in society, and these limits are not terribly confining. With a combination of planning, effort, luck, and shrewd maneuvering he can reap many shillings a day for his labor—sometimes even for other people's labor. Ashanti is not a promised land flowing with hot chocolate and honey, but neither is it a land where manna must be doled out each morning by the government. Ashanti's wealth grows steadily out of the soil, year after year, and the pound sterling fruits of the harvest are scattered over its small farms and towns.

The traditional landownership system provided—and still provides—for the communal owning of land on a community and family basis. Within each family, each man, and often some women, held the right to cultivate and to use the products of his own section as long as he wished. The major restriction on his virtual sole ownership was his lack of authority to sell, mortgage, give away, or otherwise alienate his real estate without express permission of his extended family, of his lineage—if its distant members were interested—and, if necessary, of the community chief and his council.

Theoretically, and in spirit, all Ashanti land is owned by the Asantehene, just as supreme political authority resides in him. In practice, however, just as political control is distributed down through the various levels of the hierarchy, so does control of the land devolve down from the Asantehene, through the paramount chiefs, the district and subdistrict chiefs, to the town chiefs and headmen. The land controlled by each town is distributed to its families, the headman of each family supervising the allotment of its apportioned property to the individual members of his family.

As long as an individual uses his land, it is, in effect, his, and he may bequeath it to his legitimate family heirs. If he abandons it, however, it reverts to his extended family, who will give it to another deserving family member. If a man is threatened with financial disaster, he appeals first to his family members, who are obligated, if they are able, to come to his support. Only in a dire emergency and with extreme reluctance would a family ask permission to mortgage its most precious possession, its land. The effect of this system has been to create a society of small landowners, and, while modern events are altering the pattern somewhat, the small farmer is still fairly secure as a member of a landowning family.

An innovation in landholding practices which has been steadily increasing in importance since the advent of cocoa has been individual ownership as distinct from the family control of portions of community land. Eager to extend their income-producing cocoa farms, individual farmers have culti-vated areas not falling within traditional community or family boundaries. These areas have been regarded as outside the traditional restrictions on land usage and disposal. They are bought, sold, or mortgaged, occasionally with the official regis-tration of title, more often by the unregistered but traditionally binding observance of the ritual of exchange under the surveil-lance and witness of the chief, the ancestors, and the gods. Eventually many such individually owned acres enter into the normal channels of family control through the mechanism of matrilineal inheritance at death, but during the interim there is frequent occasion for dispute and litigation over ownership.

The acquisition of large portions of land by wealthy in-vestors from other parts of Ghana also has altered the old order. Several of these in the vicinity of Goaso have either moved into previously unclaimed land or have managed to acquire rights to community or family land in exchange for favors—usually in the forms of money or influence in high places—to those in control of its distribution. These large-scale farmers usually oversee production on their farms while maintaining residence elsewhere and participate but little in the intimate affairs of the community. The scale of such ownership in and around Goaso, however, cannot be said to be so great as to constitute a problem of absentee landlordism, and the general pattern of wide distribution of landed prop-erty among smallholders is not as yet seriously threatened.

Money Grows on Trees

Kojo Mensah, about thirty-five years old and nonliterate, closely resembles many thousands of Ashanti farmers in the way in which he makes his living. He lives with his wife, children, and matrilineal family in Goaso. His ancestors were among the first to arrive here, and much of the land he farms was inherited from his mother's brother, who had inherited it from his mother's brother, and so on back through the ancestral generations. Indeed, it is the ancestors who really own his land; Mensah is merely a trustee, using the land which his ancestors have generously but temporarily placed in his hands. The Asantehene himself, who is said to "own" all the land, is only a trustee for his kingly ancestors. In Ashanti society economics is as much a religious matter as are the family, politics, or the more conventional religious activities. It is, after all, by the grace of the gods and the ancestors that all of Kojo Mensah's life is made good.

On working days, Mensah walks to his farm, nearly a mile from town, along the road which forms one of its boundaries. The other three sides are marked by rows of pineapple, separating his section from the adjacent farms of other members of his family, and providing a tasty snack for him at noon and a sweet incentive for his children when they come to work with him. Perhaps four of his approximately twelve acres are covered by uncleared forest. Two acres have been planted with cocoa seedlings, which grow for several years under the protecting shade of broad-leaved food plants like plantain and cocoyam. There are five acres of cocoa and one acre is devoted entirely to food crops. This furnishes the basic vegetables and fruits for his table, and miscellaneous garden patches scattered throughout the area help fill the larder.

The farm in no way resembles an American truck garden. It has been painstakingly hacked out of a heavy forest, a para-

dise for bushes, weeds, and vines; numerous tall trees have
been left standing for their shade, and not all of the logs or
stumps have been cleared out or burned. Although it can
hardly be seen for the trees, the farm is there, and, if the price
of cocoa only stays high or moves higher, Kojo Mensah and his
family are pleased with it—though not so pleased that the
three or four forested acres won't be cleared for cocoa as
quickly as possible.

From his garden Mensah harvests two varieties of yam,
cocoyam, plantain, cassava, eggplant, okra, a variety of beans,
red peppers, and a little corn; pineapples, bananas, and avo-
cados dress up his meals, and a few stalks of sugar cane afford
a candy reward for his children when they deserve it. The
first four of these plants provide the bulk of the diet, and all
of them are sometimes raised for export to the cities as well
as for family consumption and sale in the local market.

Continuing a long-standing pattern in the division of labor,
Mensah slashes and burns the farm out of the forest, but the
growing and distributing of foodstuffs are in the capable,
calloused hands of his wife, Afua. She tends the plants, harvests and prepares them for her husband and children, and
sells the surplus, keeping the income solely for her personal
use. This popular system gives her a most practical stake in
the family economy, offers a reward for her valuable contribution to her husband's family, to which she is joined only by
marriage, and, in favorable circumstances, affords her a financial independence which greatly strengthens her position
in both her own family and her husband's. To compensate
somewhat for the reduction in her private income as food
acreage and exports have slumped in the face of rising cocoa
production, she frequently receives an endearing, husbandly
gift of the rights to the proceeds from some cocoa acreage. Afua

works hard enough for her rewards, but she is not usually disgruntled with them.

Kojo Mensah begins his workday at about 7:00 A.M., having arisen with the sun at six o'clock to bathe, prepare himself and his tools, and depart, without breakfast, for his farm by 6:30. His only tools are a short-handled hoe, a cutlass, and a pot of palm wine to lighten the load of a day at hard, hot labor. He checks the small game traps previously set and tends the cocoa, weeding, planting, and transplanting until twelve o'clock—when the sun is directly overhead. Then he prepares his first meal of the day, usually a plantain or yam plucked and roasted over a small fire. Leisurely visiting with his neighbors or with the hired laborers he occasionally employs, he manages to avoid a return to work until about two o'clock, when he drags himself to it for another hour or two. When the sun begins to lower, he retrieves his tools and the long-empty winepot and returns home, looking forward to the relaxation of a bath, a drink, and a meal with his men friends and relatives, and a few cool evening hours of visiting with them or with his wife or playing with his children. Shortly after eight o'clock the flickering candles and kerosene lamps are dimmed, and Mensah, like the rest of Goaso, retires to his mosquito-netted bed to rest. Perhaps tomorrow there will be a legitimate reason for not going to the farm.

There is a considerable number of legitimate reasons for breaking the daily work routine. The day of the week on which he was born is a day of solemn obligation to his soul, and Thursday is a day of solemn obligation to Asase Yaa, the Earth Mother whose enormous, versatile fertility produces both spiritual and material benefits. Neither of these days should be profaned by manual labor. Then there is Sunday; although Mensah is a pagan, Sunday is the day for respect to the Christian Nyame, and in deference to Him and to his Christian friends and relatives, he avoids giving offense and stays home from work. In addition to these religious days of rest, there are others. His own gods receive daylong, special recognition four times in each six-week cycle, according to a religious calendar which decrees ceremonies at these regular intervals. Nonscheduled nonworking days occur whenever funeral observances are held, and, while he is not forced to abstain from work on those days, he would not show disrespect to the deceased or the bereaved by going to his farm. If the deceased is a relative or close friend, the weeklong period of mourning, with its enforced fasting and slow, steady ritual drinking further cuts into his working time. Personal reasons can easily be found to add to the mounting total of absentee hours. All in all, a four day, 28-hour workweek is regarded as adequate, almost as an imposition, and, since that much toil produces a fairly comfortable living, there is no sensible reason for spending more time at it. Kojo Mensah can find nothing inherently sacred or even desirable in work, and he doesn't look for it.

Work, nevertheless, although disagreeable, is necessary. There is at least a partial correlation between it and income, and when Mensah does work he does so steadily. He scoffs at the indolent who fail to reach their farms until 8:00 A.M., because they have paused for breakfast; food in the morning lies heavy in the stomach and slows the hoe. He is careful to drink just enough palm wine to lift his morale without lowering his production. He is intolerant of malingering—except, perhaps, after lunch—and the hired hand who goes to the winepot too often finds a reduction in pay at the end of the day. The wife who is persistently slow and careless may find her husband complaining to her family; his lazy children will suffer, first from tongue-lashings, later, if these don't suffice, from sharp whacks from the hand or a stick.

For all this he is not a tough boss, and the forest more often rings to the stimulating music of rhythmic work chants, accompanied by the swish and click of the hoe and cutlass, than it does to the grumbling of a disgusted manager. Work, with its heat and sweat and bugs and snakes and tough, scratching, monstrous undergrowth, has really little to recommend it, and music, as many American efficiency experts and dairy farmers also have learned, increases production and makes work more palatable. So he sings.

Cocoa farming is not itself a backbreaking job. Some foresight and patience are required, because the trees do not bear their valuable fruit for five or more years after planting. But once they begin, their pound notes can be plucked for thirty years or so without the annoyance of too much hard work. Weeding and harvesting are the most toilsome chores, and the latter occurs mainly during a three-month period beginning in October.

During the past few years, however, a worrisome cloud has hung over the cocoa farms in the nature of a dread blight, the swollen shoot disease, which has seriously reduced Ghana cocoa production in the southern regions and is currently threatening Ashanti orchards. Goaso and its neighborhood have not felt the ravages of this as yet uncurable disease of the trees, and the farmers are desperately hopeful that some means of eradicating it will be found before their area succumbs. The only method of control used thus far has been to cut out the affected trees, an extreme measure adopted by the government over the intense objections of the ruined farmers; until an effective treatment is found, there is, unhappily, no other resort. Among the less contented people now living temporarily in Goaso are those cocoa farmers from the areas to the south and east who have been reduced by the blight to working as migrant laborers on the still-prosperous western Ashanti farms.

The season of the cocoa harvest is a happy one, and, as October approaches, visions of a big pay-off, expanding expenditures, and old debt retirement motivate Kojo Mensah to intensive activity. He and his family, hired hands, and co-operative work parties—the latter much like a progressive harvesting bee—flock to the farms to cut down the golden pods, extract the brown beans, pre-ferment them, haul them to the drying racks at home, and finally bag them for delivery to the buyers' warehouse. Once the raw cocoa leaves his hands, Mensah sees no more of it until it returns from England in the form of a chocolate bar, and he, in fact, seldom tastes the end product of the process he initiated when he cleared his few acres of forest land.

Prior to 1947 the Goaso farmer had been in a weak position to bargain for prices with the European cocoa-buying firms, of which the United Africa Company—Lever Brothers in the United States is a small part of this tremendous operation—was the largest and most influential. Prices on the highly speculative world cocoa market, seasonal fluctuations in the harvest, and transportation problems helped to create a society made up of anxious, dissatisfied farmers. In the late 1930's an apparent attempt to concoct a low-price fixing agreement between the major European buyers had even provoked the farmers to a mass selling boycott of unexpected organizational and practical success. Stirred by youthful political agitators from the cities, farmers across the country demonstrated their solidarity and power by withholding delivery of their cocoa and by indirectly bringing pressure on the government to begin an inquiry into their economic affairs. Then, in 1947, the Gold Coast government created an official cocoa marketing board designed to stabilize prices throughout any one cocoa season and across the successive seasons. Since that time the European buying firms have acted primarily as handling agents, paying prices determined by the marketing board. Surpluses accumulated by the board have been held in reserve to bolster farm receipts in poor-price years. So favorable has the world cocoa market been since its establishment, however, that the marketing board, instead of having to reimburse suffering farmers in off years, has actually become a major agency for the accumulation of capital for education, welfare, and economic development, and for the control of inflation by actually holding down prices paid to the producers.

Few farmers will deny that the marketing board has stabilized their position in the economy, but Ashanti's homespun economists have some difficulty understanding just how a ceiling on their cocoa receipts improves their standard of living, even in the long run. As Kojo Mensah sees it, he would rather be stabilized upward than just stabilized. It is this understandable attitude which, in part, underlies the attempt of the Ashanti to forestall centralization of controls in a national Ghana government in which Ashanti forms a minority faction—and a comparatively wealthy and hence vulnerable minority at that.

In order to stimulate habits of saving and investment, and to provide at least a little experience in risk taking and management, the Gold Coast government organized cocoa-buying cooperatives, which have gained some, though not overwhelming, popularity in Goaso and in the Ahafo District generally. The

144

local records of the co-operative indicate that it has fallen somewhat short of its goals, for the most consistently popular feature of the co-operative has been its money-lending rather than its money-saving program. In any year, up to 75 per cent of a member's total share-capital has been available for loans and nearly 75 per cent of the members have taken full advantage of their right to borrow. A British government officer has directed the affairs of each local chapter; he has encouraged the continual purchase of share-capital and has tried to make certain that loans are used only for capital purposes, for the redeeming of old mortgages, clearing of new farms, erecting farm buildings, and buying up obligations to sell to private cocoa buyers, who have purchased their buying rights by making cash advances at high interest rates during the year. The director has had a job demanding patient vigilance, for few rural Ashanti have as yet acquired the saving habit. Incautious to a fault, from a capitalist point of view, they do not hesitate to borrow for current consumption purposes, particularly when an unexpected kinship obligation, such as a funeral, makes a sudden heavy demand on resources or when the love of leisure or heightened prestige leads a farmer to borrow in order to pay a third of his gross income to hired wage laborers or sharecroppers to do the work he himself with his family could easily do.

Many, perhaps most, of the small-scale farmers in Goaso annually find themselves at least slightly in debt, the period of greatest indebtedness coming just before the October cocoa harvest. Few of them carry a hopeless obligation from year to year—times are too good for that—but many do fall prey sooner or later to the blandishments of the private cocoa buyer who offers to tide them over if they will just promise to deliver their harvest to him. There is, of course, a "small charge" for this, but it "costs no money"; the interest charges are simply deducted from the cocoa receipts. Both parties are pleased; the farmer has his cash when he wants it and the competitive buyer has the assurance of the future cocoa delivery or, in case of forfeiture, the possibility of acquiring productive land for himself. Besides the cocoa buyers there are professional loan sharks waiting cheerfully to exploit the farmers' incaution. The loss of income to interest charges, often at a rate of 50 per cent for a term of a few months, can be staggering, and it is to offset this that the co-operatives make their offer to lend money. The disadvantage of the co-operative's program from the farmer's point of view is that it requires an approved statement of the capital-improvement purpose of the loan. The private moneylender is interested only in the repayment of his loan with interest when the cocoa ripens; a man should be allowed to spend his money as he pleases.

The records of the savings department of the cocoa co-operative also reflect Kojo Mensah's spending values. Of the amount deposited during a recent year in the current savings accounts (deposits withdrawable upon demand) nearly all was withdrawn by the end of the year, little of it for investment purposes. Not one shilling was deposited in the fixed deposit department, because this required the depositor to state a lengthy period of time during which he could not withdraw any funds. Mensah would rather stealthily bury his money in a can at the foot of a forest tree known only to him than to entrust it to some foreigner, and it is rumored—without solid confirmation—that several thousands of trees in Ashanti keep guard over several million pounds sterling. Ashanti's independent economic and political future will not be assured until Mensah disposes of his income in more productive ways.

There is not one soul in Ashanti who is not dependent, directly or indirectly, upon the cash economy that has flourished with the cocoa tree. There are, however, other types of producers in Ashanti, most of them represented in Goaso. Among them are those who earn their livings as retailers in the market places. Although most basic foodstuffs are consumed by the family that produces them, surpluses are offered for sale, especially by wives and their children, who thereby earn their private incomes, and by a variety of tradesmen. The latter, most of whom also own cocoa farms, rent market stalls from the local government where they display their inexpensive wares: soap, kerosene, salt, sugar, cosmetics, hardware, phonographs and records, flashlights, gadgets and gewgaws, dolls, toys, imported clothing in both traditional and European styles, cigarettes, matches, and the like.

In the market place, too, the butcher cuts his beef and mutton into small chunks, with a fine disregard for steaks or chops or desirable cuts which shocks the European. Beef is beef in Goaso, and brains and kidneys and tripe and sirloin bring roughly the same price after some good-natured haggling. Besieged by flies and the intense sun, the Goaso butcher longs for a refrigerated, glass-enclosed display case, but until electricity and even greater prosperity reach Goaso he must be content with his table and cool green leaves for wrapping. The butchers' trade is, by and large, in the hands of Moslems, who, though distinctly an alien minority in most of Ashanti, insist upon and receive respect for their dietary regulations, which include the kosher, ritual killing and distribution of the edible animals. Apprenticed to the butcher in Goaso is a young man who earned the right to wear his khaki military uniform while fighting totalitarianism with Goaso's European and American democratic allies in Burma during World War II.

Outside of the market place, which is usually in the center of town, are the so-called petty trade stores, which many younger men have established in the effort both to supplement their basic incomes from cocoa and to put their schooling to use in a business occupation having more prestige. The petty trade store is frequently the refuge of the young man who is qualified for clerical jobs which have long since been filled. These retailers sell, in rather desultory and not very profitable fashion, all the goods found in the market stalls, and if the shopper is thirsty he can pause for a bottle of Bavarian or Dutch or Norwegian or English or local Ghana beer—sometimes cooled in a kerosene-burning refrigerator— or for a huskier drink of schnapps or Black and White Scotch or Gordon's or Gilbey's gin. Coca-Cola may still be missing from Goaso's shelves, but the concession has already been sold to a Ghana trading company. The available drinks have passed through the clutching hands of a number of middlemen, European and African, with an effect on price which restricts the buyer from pausing too often or for too long.

Most Ashanti towns, like Goaso, diversify their production with a number of crafts owned and operated by local artisans. Goaso's craftsmen include a number of carpenters, a goldsmith, a blacksmith, two weavers, several tailors, a barber, a photographer and film developer, a butcher, a shoemaker, a sandalmaker, a number of woodcutters and sawyers, two timber contractors, a mason, and a building construction contractor. All these occupations are held by men, but women can establish themselves in business as bakers and seamstresses. Few of the craftsmen rely solely upon their business incomes, for nearly all derive the major part of their income from cocoa.

Goldsmithing, blacksmithing, and weaving were well-developed arts before the Europeans arrived in Ashanti, and they persist despite the inroads on their market made by European manufactured goods. Apprentices still serve two or three years learning a craft and working as servants in the master's household until the terms of the contract have been fulfilled, the fees paid, and they are ready to set themselves up as independent master craftsmen.

The weavers especially are still artists of distinction, working at their traditional, narrow looms, creating and copying the imaginative, intricate designs, achieving lavish effects by the use of striking juxtaposition of intense reds, greens, golds, purples, yellows, and blues. Robes so woven are still in great demand for ceremonial or other dress occasions. The cotton and silk threads are now imported from Europe, but the weavers' creations are traditional Ashanti in design, with here and there, perhaps, just a touch of alien influence. The toga-like cloths which spin from their nimble hands may be priced at well over $100, but the cost is of little moment when an Ashanti wants to emphasize the pride he takes in his people's art and culture and in the high station of life that he has reached. Colorful cotton prints, designed and manufactured in Manchester after a careful appraisal of African artistic preferences, have displaced the simpler designs and coarser weaves of the less-expensive traditional cloths for ordinary street or work wear, and, of course, many persons can afford no more than these cheaper, gay prints. But the well-dressed Ashanti must keep an ample supply of brilliant robes, beautifully woven in Ashanti by Ashanti craftsmen, neatly folded in his wardrobe, to be worn with pride and dignity on the proper occasions.

Tailors, on the other hand, work at a new occupation which caters to the growing popularity of Western styles in men's clothing. In shops equipped with pedal-operated Singer sewing machines and bolts of cotton and woolen materials, they will fit a man with safari shorts, with a cotton undershirt excellent for farm work, with a distinguished three-piece suit for that modern look, or with a white broadcloth shirt to complete the ensemble. Seamstresses, on their hand-powered machines, perform a similar service for women, although their conservative tastes run to more moderate alterations of the traditional styles. The addition of a modest blouse to their already modest garb, consisting of a toga-like dress with a wrap-around at the waist, has largely satisfied Goaso's feminine desires for a slightly new look in clothing. Ashanti men are not forced to indulge their women in annual revisions of silhouette, hemline, and decolletage. So long as a new dress, if in a familiar mode, is forthcoming two or three times a year, a Goaso wife is both fashionable and pleased with her husband.

The goldsmith, having completed his apprenticeship, selects a likely, prosperous town and opens a shop at his residence. His tools are few and simple: an earthen hearth, a hand-pumped bellows and a small boy to pump it, several molds, instruments for handling the molten metal and the delicate designs, and an oil burner. During most of the year he occupies himself with designing and manufacturing jewelry —all the while keeping one eye on his cocoa farm and the hired hands who tend it—in preparation for the big seasons when money is most plentiful and husbands and sweethearts most susceptible. Christmas, falling providentially well within the cocoa harvest, and Easter are the times of the year when feminine desires for gifts of jewelry coincide with masculine abilities to satisfy those desires.

These craftsmen, with the exception of the seamstresses who are unorganized, usually belong to craft guilds, membership in which is open to master craftsmen on an Ashanti-wide basis. The connections of Goaso's artisans with these guilds are somewhat tenuous, Goaso being rather far from the large towns. In more populous centers they operate in several capacities to represent the craftsmen to the government—goldsmiths need gold and other precious metals which come under rigid government regulation—to determine and enforce standards of workmanship, and to control the conditions of apprenticeship.

The guilds have the additional brotherly social function of providing the spiritual and financial benefits of a fraternity, lodge, or mutual aid society. At death, for example, the guild members assist in the performance of funeral rites and share the funeral expenses of deceased brothers; they may lend money or tools or supplies in a crisis, or entertain visiting or traveling members. Although retail prices are not directly controlled by the guild, they can come under its surveillance, and an unscrupulous price cutter might encounter difficulty obtaining supplies or might at least lose his personal relationship with comrades in the guild, a serious loss in view of the intimate social as well as economic functions of the group.

An artisan conspicuously absent from the Goaso manufacturing trades is the wood carver, a specialist who once could be found in most villages but is now disappearing from the job classification lists. The Ashanti are not prominent among those West African peoples who burst quite suddenly on the European art world early in this century by virtue of their aggressively styled, dramatically expressive carvings of masks and human figures. Having confined himself largely to the production of distinctive wooden stools, which served as the primary piece of furniture in the household, the Ashanti carver has left relatively less imprint on the canvases and sculptures of modern Europe than have his neighbors to east and west. Nevertheless, his was an esteemed position in the old Ashanti, and a sentimental observer might be forgiven for mourning his passing. His near demise is not mourned, however, by the Ashanti, who have accepted in his place the carpenter, who saws and planes and hammers out furniture of European design in the simpler, unimaginative styles of mail-order houses. Following the patterns of blueprints and mail-order catalogues, he turns out chairs and benches, tables and desks, beds and chests of drawers to suit the current tastes in furniture of modern Goaso.

Through such secondary economic activities as these, Goaso has diversified its production to a small degree. Local or neighboring markets, however, consume most of this production, and none of it is manufactured for export out of the area. For its real wealth Goaso is utterly dependent upon cocoa, and its dependence thus far has been highly rewarding. By and large, the people of Goaso are fairly well off when compared to the people in most nonindustrialized parts of the world. Nearly all the people of Goaso agree that their standard of living is far superior to anything they enjoyed in pre-British times. They would not willingly part with the tangible rewards of their good fortune, their more peaceful society, their improved housing, their roads and schools and clothing, the medical services, their longer life and better health, and the large inventory of European goods they have come to desire and to afford because of their cocoa incomes. Their anti-

British-imperialist political views are tempered considerably by an optimism which foresees steadily increasing incomes—at the worst, no diminution of incomes—and, so far as economic production and the enjoyment of material things is concerned, the people of Goaso look with some pity upon their less fortunate, born-too-soon ancestors.

Colonies have primarily been enjoyed by their imperial controllers for their extracted raw materials, for their cheap labor, and for the markets they provide for finished goods. Goaso has, in fact, provided all of these, but not by any means to its complete detriment. For, as a largely unforeseen by-product of its cocoa wealth, of the associated social changes which the British have encouraged and permitted, and of the correlated social changes which both the British and the Africans are powerless to stop, Goaso is providing many members of the present generation of empire administrators with a new source of satisfaction. It is the knowledge of having guided Ashanti and Ghana toward a surprisingly rapid realization of self-government. Not all the British take pride in this accomplishment—development would have been much more gradual had Africans been less insistent. And the enjoyment of many British is tempered by apprehension of the possible future failure of the self-government experiment. Nevertheless, in less than two generations of cocoa trees, the culturally hybrid Ghana has grown to vigorous if as yet youthful, not quite certain maturity.

9. The Wider World

Prosperity comes from planting and harvesting, from a lush cocoa crop and high prices, from the fortunate interplay of all those social, economic, and political forces which a man may try to manipulate; prosperity is worked for and earned. But at the same time, in the same breath, in the same thought, prosperity is the token of a good soul; success is the gift of a strong, protecting spirit, the symbol of the approval of benign, well-satisfied ancestors, of the benediction of the gods, of adequate control over sorcerers and ill-willed spirits. Children, long life, vigorous health, happy marriages, a stable society, and all other good things are but reflections of a state of harmony and unity existing between the seen world and the unseen.

Prosperity is not earned solely by the simple, direct application of brawn or by the shrewd calculations of the brain. For there is a visible world and an invisible world, but they are not two worlds; they are one world, and the good things of this world are obtained only when this is understood. Because of this unity, an Ashanti engrossed in politics or family affairs or earning a living is also participating in his religion; an Ashanti engrossed in religion is engaged in political action or family life or economic affairs. In modern Ashanti, as in Europe or America, these worlds are gradually being rent

154

asunder, compartmentalized, but Ashanti is not yet England or the United States, and the sacred and secular aspects of life are not yet so easily divisible. Certain clusters of beliefs and practices, however, can be viewed as predominantly religious rather than predominantly economic or political or social, and they may, therefore, be discussed separately. But the farmer who works for his prosperity does not, in addition, also pray for his prosperity; his work and his prayers are integral parts of the same act.

Because of the fine, gray, really invisible line drawn between the seen and the unseen world, it is not surprising to learn of the Ashanti fundamental belief in the soul. Perhaps a little more startling is the belief that all people have not one but two souls. Some Ashanti maintain that there are three souls, but the difference between two and three souls is not a crucial one. As a matter of fact, the difference between one soul and two souls is primarily important to those who believe in but one soul. Few Ashanti would care to argue seriously about it, since souls are largely invisible and thus difficult to count. Assuming two souls, then, the Ashanti have worked out their beliefs about them in a manner which satisfactorily answers the particular questions about life which Ashanti ask.

It is possible that the two souls are but two aspects of a single soul which function in slightly different ways. One aspect, the *kra*, is a superpersonal soul, placed in the first men by Nyame, the Supreme Creator, and since that time transmitted through human fathers to their children. The second soul, or soul-aspect, which may be called "spirit," is the *sunsum*; it is similarly received through the father, but it serves primarily as a protector or escort of the soul and of the person. The soul is eternal; the spirit mortal, dying with the body as the shadow of a man disappears when he dies.

It will be recalled that a child belongs to his mother's family. He does so because he is formed from the blood of his mother. But what is it that gives life to this otherwise inert fluid? The Ashanti are fully cognizant of the mechanics of conception—if not of the biology of it—but, as may be expected of a religious and philosophical people, they do not confuse mere mechanics with causation. For their explanation of the miracle of conception they turn to an appropriate miraculous causal reality, the soul. It is the soul, or *kra*, of the father that gives life to the blood of the mother. A child, therefore, belongs to his mother's family because he is made from her blood, which is the blood of her mother; he belongs to his father and his father's father because from them he has received his soul, which is life. Every child is thus truly the child of his parents.

Because the number of men first created by Nyame was limited—as was the number of women—the number of inheritable souls is likewise limited—as is the number of Ashanti matrilineal clans. Since a name has been given to each of the souls, all persons having a soul of the same name feel akin to each other, and, if they are unusually devoted to traditional religious customs, observe together certain taboos on behavior. The name of a person's soul is not inherited from the father along with the soul itself, for the name of the soul is derived from the day of the week on which the child is born. The farmer, Kojo Mensah, was born on a Monday, for that is what Kojo means; his wife, Afua, was born on Friday; Kojo's father, Kofi, was born on Friday; his sister, Ajowa, on Monday, like himself.

Far from being an uncomfortable piece of eternity imprisoned for a few mortal years in a fleshly, human shell, the soul intensely involves itself in the direction of life. It protects the individual and promotes his general welfare. It extends its care beyond the individual to his wife and family, thus assuming tremendous responsibility for marital accord, marriage stability, and childbearing and rearing. Like men, women have souls, received through their fathers, but the soul of a woman is constitutionally weaker than that of a man; it is dependent, subordinate, continually seeking the support and care of a soul stronger than itself. Until she marries a girl lives under the protection of her father's soul; at marriage the bride departs from the soul of her father and passes into the comforting care of her husband's soul, where she remains until widowed or divorced.

Although it normally resides in the body through which it is diffused, the soul can dissociate itself from the body, as it does in dreams, when it can travel to far places and engage in clandestine adventures, or as it does in death, when it journeys to the ancestral world. The soul may also take wings on occasions when a person feels especially expansive or powerful, when the sense of confidence or well-being is strong within a man. More disturbing, though, are those flights in the dark of the night, when the restless or perverse soul leaves the body to flit about on the nefarious missions of witches, spearing through the air like a flame to inflict injury, illness, or death. The soul of the woman who appears to be sleeping peacefully at her husband's side may in actuality be miles away, secretly cavorting with other souls or conniving with them at sorcery or skulduggery.

Personality and psychological processes are explained by the soul and its activities—emotions, sensation, perception, memory, insight, thinking, the gathering, storing, sorting, and combining of knowledge; all these are the province of the soul. A person whose soul exercises masterful control over

157

them is a wise and good man, while the actions of the stupid or immoral or emotionally explosive man reflect a weak soul. When heated or angered by insults to the person or his dignity, the soul must be cooled by the private, individual performance of a ritual of pacification, in which the person addresses his soul as represented by those most precious, intimate possessions which have been secreted in a personal container stored in his room. Hot and restless during youth, the soul may seek its shortsighted satisfactions in excessive sexual pleasures, but as the young man acquires the wisdom and experience of maturity the desires of his soul turn to the fathering of children, who, of all pleasures, bring the deepest satisfactions. In the Ashanti catechism, man is, above all, a soul.

In many respects the *sunsum*, or spirit, is so identical with the *kra*, or soul, in its functions that it is difficult to distinguish between them. It is clearly different, however, in that it is not restricted to human beings, as is the soul. The gods, for example, have a heavy spirit, and in this lies much of the superiority of their power over men. Certain trees are known to possess their own spirit, as do some animals, like the elephant, leopard, and goat. Certain rocks, stones, or hills—usually striking in appearance—may also contain it. If the spirit of the gods is heavier than that of men, however, the spirit of such animate or inanimate, nonhuman things is light, lighter even than the spirit of women. Still, it is spirit and must be respected and reckoned with. When a tree is felled or an animal killed, its spirit—if it has one—must be placated, so that it may never wreak revenge upon the human being who has destroyed it. Most plants and animals are without spirit—or, better, they have spirit of such little weight that it can be disregarded. Insects, for example, have no appreciable spirit; for all practical purposes, they are just bugs.

Nevertheless, through the concept of spirit the Ashanti achieve a unified view of a world, all of which shares somehow in a powerful, living force. The world of nature, the world of man, the world of the gods and ancestors, the world of the creator-god, Nyame, these are one world. In the Ashanti catechism the real world is a soul-world, the soul-world a real world. And they are one world.

At the death of the body in which it has lived the spirit is no more. The soul, however, never falters at death. Throughout life this aspect of the living force within each person, derived from Nyame, the Supreme Creator, has sustained the integrity and well-being of the individual and his immediate family, and has expressed its own individual nature through the personality of its possessor. Now, at death, the soul maintains the continuity between the seen world of the living and the unseen world of the ancestral dead which was earlier demonstrated at its birth. The body departs to the grave, the spirit dissolves to nothingness, but the soul takes up a different, though not really new, life. It remains essentially itself, but it is called by a new name, *saman*, reflecting its changed function as it lives among the ancestral souls, the *asamanfo*, instead of among living mortal men.

Its journey from this life to the "other life" is symbolized in the rituals of the burial and funeral, and most souls make the transition gradually, directly, and without mishap. A few souls, however, find it necessary to pass through an intermediate state before reaching the ancestral world, or *asamando*. Such an unfortunate soul—and he is to be pitied—is called a *sasa*, a restless, temporarily homeless, stateless soul. He is in this predicament because an abnormal death started him on his ancestral journey on the wrong foot; he may have suffered death through an unexplained disease or through sorcery, through accident or violence, or he may have died so far from home that his family knew nothing of it or was unable for some reason to provide a proper burial and funeral rites. Rootless, the restless soul roams the earth searching for peace, and in this unhappy condition he may reveal his plight by becoming visible from time to time—as a ghost—or, invisible, he may pursue the living with his urgent, annoying, even dangerous pleas for help until identified by a priest-diviner.

One such soul of recent memory was a young man killed when the truck in which he was riding overturned. For three days the soul hung about, pestering a surviving cousin to join him in death, "to taste death to see if it is a good thing." The cousin, greatly preferring the taste of a life enriched with cocoa, attempted to fend off his persistent relative with a magical potion of the home-remedy type; this failing, he consulted a priest, who prescribed the offering of a sacrificial lamb for the pacification of the restless soul. Apparently appeased, the soul withdrew his morbid invitation and in time became a healthy, well-adjusted ancestral soul.

Life among the ancestors differs from that among men primarily in that the participants are disembodied and deathless. Otherwise, the ancestral world is a society of Ashanti men and women and children with a structure like that of living Ashanti society, with its restrictions and frustrations, its pleasures and satisfactions, its families and classes, its royalty and free commoners and slaves, its politics and courts, and all that makes Ashanti proud.

It is not a world apart; it is an invisible society of men which participates in the visible society of men. Indeed, the ancestors are the true owners of property, the true heads of the family, the true rulers of the state. Living men who serve as family heads or chiefs or kings, controlling property and lives and administering the affairs of society, are but the temporal representatives of the ancestors; it is the ancestors who own and direct and who provide the sanction for all temporal authority. Living men are by no means puppets dangling at the ends of strings, manipulated by omnipotent ancestors behind the scenes. Men are free to represent their ancestors well or badly. But if they wish to succeed, to enjoy the good, proud life, they must learn to dance to ancestral drums. Because the ancestors are so thoroughly immanent in society, so powerful in the affairs of men, they receive the recognition, respect, and veneration which all people holding true authority receive in any society.

The term "ancestor worship" has been applied to this kind of belief and behavior. Because this is a term easily misunderstood and ridiculed or pitied, it is perhaps better to substitute for it a phrase like "reverence for ancestors and respect for history." This is essentially what "ancestor worship" means—or ought to mean. Far from being a stupid superstition—as it is frequently regarded by societies which deliver their ancestors to a rather remote, if extremely pleasant, kingdom of heaven—it is a philosophical, religious affirmation of the unity between the visible, present world of living men and the invisible, historic past which continues to exert its influence upon present events. It is, to be sure, the kind of affirmation made by a society which is oriented toward traditions, dedicated to preserving the way of life that has provided a people with dignity and satisfaction and stability for many generations. It also reflects the thinking of a people who delight in the personification of things, in the personalizing of abstractions, in the supernaturalizing of events. But this does not detract from its usefulness. Quite the contrary, this belief in the ancestors is the foundation of such practical rights as the right to continuous ownership of property, the right to political office, the right to membership in a family, the right to participate freely in a society of men, the right of inadequate men to enjoy the protection and help of the more adequate supernatural. These are rights which must somehow be guaranteed to the members of any society. The Ashanti believe that the guarantors take the spiritual form of ancestors, but this is only a special, conservative way of saying that the roots of any man, any society, take their nourishment from the soil of the past.

The ancestors are not faring so well these days. Under the tutelage of the British and through increasing awareness of the Western, democratic political systems, the Ashanti have learned that there are other means of ensuring rights to life, property, and power. In their own homeland, the British and even some Americans continue to make symbolic use of the lineage of their ancestors, but by and large social rewards in the Western democracies are conferred upon those who either struggle successfully or contrive successfully to win them. The appeal of such a system of distributing rewards, associated as it is with other economic, social, and religious changes in Ashanti society, has created considerable uncertainty in the visible world about the value of the invisible world. It appears now that the ancestors are retreating in some confusion, and with them the traditional safeguards to all the individual and social rights they have long sustained. It is to be hoped that they will not be completely vanquished.

A society which tries completely to ignore its ancestors falls heir to a social inheritance of dwindling personal satisfactions and mounting interpersonal tensions.

The Ashanti have more than their ancestors to rely upon in time of trouble or overwhelming desire; they have their gods. It is a good thing, too, especially for Goaso, whose ancestors are not numbered among the first rank and who are, therefore, less potent than is desirable. Goaso has its ancestors, but even more it has its gods, who stand ready to receive the thanksgiving and the supplications of their children. Foremost among them and arching over all the gods is Nyame (en-yah-may), the Supreme Creator.

Nyame is sometimes thought to be the sky; at least he is somehow identified with the sky, although actually the sky is no more Nyame than the sky is blue. Nyame is the fathomless spirit who has made all creation. He once was very close to earth and its people, but he became annoyed when struck repeatedly by a woman pounding fufu with a large mortar and pestle. With the words—or so one account has it—"You mortals, when I am close to you, you try to hurt me; I shall leave you" he departed to his present distant location, where he maintains an attitude of interested aloofness. His is not a sulking, pathetic remoteness, however, for among his creatures he has left witnesses to himself and to his continuing care for men and for the whole of his creation. These are the gods who are the intermediaries between Nyame and men and who, more than Nyame, provide the day-to-day assurances that men are not alone in the world. The manner in which Nyame has achieved his purposes is here told by a priest of one of these gods in Goaso.

"Nyame came first and covered the sky. Then he created Asase, the earth. Next he created rivers and waters; then plants and trees to drink from the waters. Then man to make use of the things he had created. After man he created animals for man to use. Then he made food; he ordered animals to eat the plants, and he ordered man to do the same, and to drink from the waters; he also ordered man to use the animals as meat. Lastly he created the gods to protect man; some of these come from waters, some from the forest and the rocks. The gods themselves reveal their taboos and punish serious infraction of them by killing the offender.

"Nyame created the world as it is in a way which ensures harmony and order; and he created the gods in order to bring peace and protection and contentment to everyone and important positions to a few, such as the priests. Nyame has made everyone to perform each his own work; the priest has his, the Christian church member has his. Because Nyame thought it wise that everyone should perform his own work, he created things in an ordered fashion. If a man envies another's work and tries to take it from him, the gods and Nyame are angered because the order is broken. If any man fails to do his appointed work, he can expect no help from Nyame and the gods.

"Nyame's greatest taboo is evil. It is true, nonetheless, that he has created the possibility of evil in the world; that is, he has created evil, but not people to be evil. Before people are born, they tell Nyame what ideas and opinions they will hold and what actions they will perform; he permits them all of these; he does not force his will upon them. Thus some people ask that their lives be short so that they may soon return to the ancestral world; they may be killed by a falling tree or by drowning. In the same way, some tell him that they will live an evil life; that is, a life contrary to what most people know to be good. Everyone knows the difference between these two ways, for Nyame has created the knowledge of good and evil in every person and allowed him to choose his way. An evil man may have a long life, if he has asked Nyame for it, but he cannot successfully escape his punishment; his retribution comes when he returns to Nyame and the ancestral world, for, just as there is punishment for people in this world, there is punishment among the ancestors for evil deeds."

Nyame is respected and venerated, but he is not usually worshiped. He is mentioned unobtrusively in prayers, but for the most part he is thought of only in a general way, as the great creator who stands behind his creation without involving himself in specific mundane events, yet watchful in all of them.

Second only to Nyame in power is the first of his creations, Earth, personified as the fertile, great-breasted goddess, Asase Yaa. Through her, Nyame has created their children, the rocks, the forests, the hills, the springs and streams and pools of water, the plants and animals, and the supernatural personalities and powers often associated with many of them. Like Nyame, she receives little specific ritual recognition, although her day, Thursday, is respected, and the earth on that day lies in quiet rest, untrammeled, unturned. She well deserves her rest, for from this fecund woman spring all the things of the earth which sustain the life of man, and all men know that without her lavish bounty they could not live.

Of all the children of Asase Yaa, the Tano River in western Ashanti is the most beneficial to men, for it is in the deeps of the Tano that the major gods have revealed themselves. Other gods, too, have sprung from Asase Yaa's fertile loins, from her forests and high hills and from other rivers and streams, and no town or village has been left without her help and through her the help of Nyame.

Goaso has received the revelation of two such gods, Te Kofi Nentiya, who first presented himself to the people of Goaso in the Tano River, and Bonsam, the child of a powerful forest god, Sasabonsam. Separately and together they serve the people of Goaso and any other persons who wish to appeal to them for aid. Nentiya and Bonsam do not compete with each other for the favor of Goaso; both perform the same functions, both possess the same powers, each aids the other in their healing, protecting work. Bonsam refers to Nentiya as "father," because Nentiya revealed himself earlier in Goaso's history, and he kneels before the senior god in ceremonies, but their real relationship is that of intimate brothers, each of whom reveres the other.

Goaso suffers no disruptive religious competition, in large part because neither of its gods has established a church or cult. They are the coequal gods of Goaso; they are one in the work they do, and the people of Goaso accept both of them for what they have claimed and proved themselves to be. There is no cult membership, no concerted drive for adherents, no advertising, no subscription campaigns; the gods are simply available for those who wish to acknowledge their dependence upon them and to use them for the general welfare of Goaso and Ashanti and for the specific welfare of individuals. Most of the people of Goaso do so—or did so before the aliens brought a somewhat different conception of god and a changed way of life.

The royal family of Goaso has the obligation of caring for the god Nentiya, and it may be said that this lineage owns him. His blessings, however, are bestowed upon the members of the community served by the royal family and are withheld from none who seek them properly. Politics and religion are not separate compartments of life in Goaso. In keeping with his political role, a god publicly assumes obligations to his people at the time of his revelation; he swears that he will answer when called, that he will hear and respond to their requests for help and health and prosperity, for protection against sorcerers, ill-willed spirits, and against all harm to the community. The citizens in turn pledge themselves to obey his commandments and prescriptions and to give him the homage that is his divine due.

From time to time a god may achieve such a pinnacle of success that his fame spreads throughout Ashanti and even into other parts of Ghana or into neighboring countries. This has been particularly the case during the past few decades of social upheaval, when many persons, socially and emotionally upset by changing cultural forces they cannot easily understand or master, have attributed their problems to the perverse activities of sorcerers. A number of shrewd gods have managed to create the impression that they can successfully identify and either kill or purge these demons, and their popularity has soared along with their bank accounts—a not-surprising religious development in an era when a society, in normal times satisfactorily equipped with a ready explanation in sorcery for personal and social ills, enters upon an abnormal period of rapid social change and an enormous increase in problem situations.

Most local gods, however, conduct their affairs in a steadier, less spectacular, less exploitative manner. A god assures his regional popularity by means of a run of good fortune, by making barren women conceive, by accurately predicting such events as death or economic success, by prescribing effective cures for illness or anxiety, or by any other impressive demonstration of his power. Most gods can survive even a series of mediocre performances, but if one should prove utterly ineffective in his appointed work, the people turn to other gods. No blame accrues to the god for this apparent desertion of his children; on the contrary, it is believed quite simply, even indifferently, that he has withdrawn himself from intimate contact with human affairs because he is angered at man's evil behavior or because of other sufficient reasons known only to him.

This reaction to abandonment by the gods reflects a major emphasis in Ashanti theology upon the function of gods in human life rather than upon the theological elaboration of their essential natures. No god need justify his existence to men through his acts, for he was not created by men; a god is in no way eternally obligated to serve them. But his existence is of little interest to men unless he actively plays a beneficent role in their lives. If a god wishes to go, let him go. There are other gods who will listen and help; men are not in a state of utter dependence upon a single god. Nyame has left many witnesses to his power and goodness.

The gods reveal themselves and make themselves available to mortals through men or women whom they specially call to be their priests and spokesmen. Frequently these are descendants or near relatives of ordained priests, though the gods are not limited in their selection to family or lineage members. The divine call comes quite suddenly and persuasively, but confirmation of its legitimacy rests with the community served by the gods as well as with the individual who claims to have received the divine command. To protect the town against ne'er-do-wells and fakers, who may be called primarily by a burning desire for a fairly good, easy living in the religious vocation, a claimant undergoes the rigid, skeptical scrutiny of the headmen of the town and of other priests. He is screened for such factors as satisfactory family background, health, intelligence, aptitude for the vocation, moral character, sobriety, and general knowledge of the requirements of the priestly profession. If these informal examiners are convinced that this is not a counterfeit call, the applicant is pronounced ready to take the training which will make him a bona fide priest. Once he has passed this test, and the conviction of his legitimate calling is shared by the people, he takes special vows of service to the gods and to the community he will serve and enters into a prolonged period of training.

For three or four years he remains under the tutelage of a priest either of the god who has called him or of some other god—for the gods know each other well and can substitute for each other in the training of an apprentice. During these years he learns the theology and the rituals, the songs, the dances, and the drumming; he learns the sacred myths and stories and history, the kinds of behavior which are required or prohibited by the god, which please or displease him, the secret, esoteric knowledge and the special, ceremonial, secret language of the gods, the techniques for divining and the interpretation of signs and symbols, the diagnosis of illnesses and the prescriptions for cures, the insight and wisdom that can solve personal problems and relieve anxiety. When the neophyte has completed his theological training he is presented to the community at an exciting ceremony in which the god himself expresses approval of his servant through an awesome display of power. The uninitiated "objective" spectator may be unaware of anything unusual occurring in the ceremony, but the conviction of the participants that "the spirit was here" cannot be denied. And so Te Kofi Nentiya and Bonsam have called and ordained their priests.

In all the crucial periods of life, during pregnancy, at birth, during the tense years of childhood when life hangs in the balance, during illness and at death, the god is with his people, protecting, comforting, reassuring, and sometimes condemning. Between times, too, he is present. There may be no daily formal recognition of the god's nearness, but he is there— unless, of course, some particular god has withdrawn himself for some particular reason, as a god is now and then wont to do; gods, after all, have a life of their own to live. Ordinarily there is little question that the god is nearby, anxious to do whatever he can to care for his children and servants.

Public ceremonies for the god are held each nine days, and on these days his presence is acclaimed with a ritual pageantry varying in its elaborateness according to the priest, the prosperity, and the religious interest of the community. Some ceremonies appear meager, indeed, but others would suit the highest of high gods. Regardless of the degree of pomp and circumstance, all ceremonies have two major purposes: to relieve the anxieties of troubled souls who come to the god for help and to dramatize the protection he freely offers his children. Nentiya and Bonsam, Goaso's gods, perform both to the satisfaction of at least half of Goaso's people.

The priest of Bonsam appears as a rather foreboding, threatening man, but his appearance is deceptive only to those who know neither him nor what to look for in an Ashanti priest. He is, in fact, reflective, responsible, possessed of a sense of humor and self-perspective which enables him to play a serious role without overbearing seriousness. Dressed as a layman rather than as priest or god, the one visible mark of his religious calling is the length of his plaited hair, one of the symbols of the god for whom he is a priest; as Bonsam wears his hair long, so must his priest, and so he has foresworn the close-cropped style of other men. The toga he wears is a cotton print, manufactured in England, one of the innumerable vivid patterns popular with African men and women.

If Bonsam, the very god, bears a striking resemblance to the priest, it is only because the god chooses to reveal himself in the form of a man whom he has called for that purpose. But the two, man and god, are not to be confused with each other, for the priest is a man, the god is the god. Each ninth day Bonsam, the god, makes his scheduled appearance, clothing his invisible, spiritual self in a visible, material body by possessing or infusing himself into the person of the priest. On this day the priest wears the special vestments and decorations of his god—the grass skirt, the white clay pigment which covers his body, the bells and charms suspended about his neck and entwined about his arms, legs, and chest; in his hands he carries the symbols of the god's awesome power, the sword in his left hand and the cowtail switch in his right, with which dangers and fears are cut down and whisked away. Attending the god are his special servants, who care for his sacred wants, prepare the temple area for his dancing, and translate the esoteric language of the god when he speaks—a ceremonial language which has been identified as an archaic dialect of Twi, a modern dialect of which is spoken by the Ashanti, most of whom profess not to understand the ceremonial speech of the god. In mystery and strength, in understanding and tenderness, comes Bonsam, fearless destroyer of fear, mighty defender of his people.

Bonsam greets his people at a small one-room temple on the edge of town. Ceremonies for Nentiya are held in the courtyard of the home, belonging to the royal family, in which the sacred symbols of that god are kept in state. On certain occasions ceremonies for both gods may occur on the same day; then Bonsam, the younger god, goes to Nentiya's temple to greet him in a manner appropriate to the latter's senior position.

Drums beat the nervous, supplicating rhythms of the invocation as mounting, suspenseful tension warns of the approach of the god. Bonsam hears them, as if faintly at first; he hesitates, then begins to respond to the urgent call of his children who have gathered to pay him homage. The drums have been anointed with white clay, and their spirits have been fed and elevated with the offering of an egg smashed upon the body of the drum—for the world of spirit and of matter is not divisible—and the drummers work professionally, coolly, and efficiently at their instruments, cajoling, enticing, calling the god with the music they know pleases him. Moved by the drums' stimulating beat, he comes closer, and the priest begins to tremble, the bells and rattles which adorn his body luring the god on with their sweet sounds. Then, suddenly, Bonsam has appeared, and the person of the entranced priest fades into the person of the god.

As the complicated rhythms change from supplication to praise of the great protector and benefactor of the people, he begins to speak, but the words are in a strange tongue, the language of the gods. The choir of women, seated in a place of quiet honor at one side of the temple arena, chant their hymns to the mighty god, to him who brings children to women, who cures the illnesses of the body and the soul, who provides all good things. After the god has walked with gracious dignity about the temple area greeting the worshipers, he takes his seat upon an elaborate, brass-studded chair placed on a dais in front of the temple and invites the people to approach him.

Those who wish press forward to address him humbly with their petitions for help or with their testimonies to his goodness. As each speaks, Bonsam, analyzing the present and divining the future, peers through a clay-whitened stone ring, which, the priest explains, snaps a picture of the unseen through the aperture, operating much as does an ordinary camera. The music softens but seldom dies, now and then swelling in a crescendo of joyous emotion as the ritual rewards those who trust their god.

The words of the supplicants, uttered sometimes in awe, sometimes in smug satisfaction, sometimes in simple gratitude, sometimes in fearful desperation, reveal those aspects of life in Goaso which bring the greatest anxieties and the greatest joys. At one ceremony, the god consulted on such matters as these:

A father, cuddling an infant in his arms, thanked Bonsam for answering his request for a child. The child was now suffering from dysentery, and the father felt he must beseech the god to help in curing it. Bonsam prescribed that the mother refrain from going to the farm for one day, that she devote all her time to the child and sleep with it that night. Within a few days, Bonsam assured him, the child would be completely well.

An old man asked how he would fare generally during the remainder of his years. Bonsam reminded him of the many children in his family who would care for him, but warned him to be wary of one of them who was jealous of him.

A pregnant woman thanked Bonsam for giving her a child and sought protection for herself and for the child she was about to bear. Bonsam, pleased, gave her his benediction by touching white clay to her abdomen and assured her of an easy childbirth.

A woman, accompanied by a boy of about sixteen years, complained that the young man was spending too much money, a fault she attributed to some unspecified evil influences. Bonsam agreed with her diagnosis and promised that he would try to protect the boy from these distractions; he could not assure her of success.

Several small children and infants were presented to Bonsam for a blessing which would protect them from illness and accidental harm. He was happy to grant it. Twin girls, four years old, were presented to Bonsam and the congregation as evidence of Bonsam's goodness, for twins are a sure sign that a family is twice blest.

A young mother brought a sick, wasting infant for whom she desired a prognosis. A hesitant Bonsam, peering carefully through his divination stone ring, regretfully advised her that the child could not be cured, that there was no hope for him, that she needed a strong tree to lean upon. The distraught woman pleaded that there was no better help than Bonsam; she appealed to him to save the child. Bonsam softly dismissed her, saying there was nothing he could do in this instance, but she remained nearby and returned again to plead with him. Finally the god directed her to bring the child later that day to the home of Bonsam's priest, who would tell her what might be done for the child. She retired, somewhat more hopeful than before.

A mother with a sick child was told that one year from this day the child would be well enough to come along to thank Bonsam for his good health.

A woman who wanted a child was warned that she should

not seek to conceive through consultation with any other god but Bonsam or through charms procured from any Moslem. If she did conceive in this way, it would result in death during pregnancy.

The mother of a teen-age son asked help in curing her son of a penchant for stealing, for she well knew that, if he did not stop, the "red ones"—the police—would lock him in jail. Bonsam replied that a certain evil influence was forcing him into crime, that if the child was bathed three times a day in water containing a formula the priest would prepare, the thieving would be stopped.

A man complained that some money had been stolen from his home. The god advised him that within two weeks the culprit would become ill, would confess his crime to the god, and would be directed to return the money and to pacify Bonsam, who felt personally insulted and angered by the crime.

A man from a neighboring town came forward to state that he was donating a sheep to Bonsam in gratitude for a remarkably prosperous year.

A man testified that a god he had consulted in another town had informed him that he was well protected by Bonsam and Nentiya, both of whom followed him solicitously wherever he went.

So the petitioners and worshipers bring their fears and pleasures before the trembling, awesome god, seeking good counsel, expressing honest gratitude. When they have finished, Bonsam rises in his place, now excited more and more by the increasingly agitated, irresistible, staccato rattle of the drums. With dignity he steps from the dais and slowly, at first, begins to dance; as the tempo and volume increase, his movements become more vigorous, until finally the intricate, twisting, striding, turning steps of his solo dance drama carry him rapidly about the temple arena. A skilled dancer, he has partly learned and partly created a choreography which dramatizes the relationships between Bonsam and the people of Goaso. The symbolic meanings of his dance patterns and the virtuosity of his performance persuade them again that their god is a sure defense, a help in time of trouble. When the people have witnessed once more how great is their god, he slowly takes his departure.

The body of the god, exhausted after perhaps two hours of constant trembling, strenuous dancing, and emotion-sapping divination, is transformed slowly into that of the priest, a tired man who needs rest and refreshment after the prolonged ordeal through which he has just gone. The priest retires with a few servants into the inner chamber of the temple to remove the vestments of the god and to relax, the drummers return with their instruments to their homes, the crowd disperses, and the humble, elderly, female servants devoutly sweep the arena with their palm branches, so that all may know it is a fitting abode for the mighty Bonsam until he returns again.

Goaso's gods, like all Ashanti gods, are superhuman persons, but they do not possess the omnipotence with which many of the world's gods are invested. Bonsam's prescriptions and predictions, for example, do not always prove to be correct. For these miscalculations there are explanations. A god is, after all, only a god. He wrestles with unseen forces and conditions nearly as powerful, sometimes more powerful than he. He is essentially a person; stronger, more moral, greater than men, but nevertheless a person. He is certainly not an irresistible force, whose whim is sheer power, whose mere fancy can predetermine events. He lives and works in a fluid, changing situation; he has no timeless perspective on the world. He is subject to many of the limitations of finite men, though always in lesser degree. If, then, he proves sometimes to be weak or in error, what of it? What religious person denies the reality of God because of an unanswered prayer? Bonsam's failures are attributed to a god's partial limitations rather than to man's limited understanding of the inscrutable, infinite wisdom of a god. His intentions are always right and good; one can expect no more of an infinite god. Besides, Bonsam is right more than half the time, for Goaso is a small community and Bonsam is experienced and wise; he knows his community too well to be wrong very often. And, if by chance he is often wrong, anyone can understand that he has withdrawn from men. And if Bonsam retires, Te Kofi Nentiya remains.

One need no more question the honesty or sincerity of the priests of Bonsam or Nentiya than of any religious who speaks for the supernatural in any religion. Certainly the Ashanti pagan does not question the integrity of the Christian or Moslem practitioner. In his view Nyame, the creator, can and does reveal himself in many ways to many people; Jehovah and Allah are two such revelations. Bonsam and Nentiya are two others of a different sort. There is no need to be disturbed by this variety. More than one Christian church has benefited by the donations from Ashanti priests and other non-Christians, and the coexistence of Christian and pagan practice is almost everywhere harmonious, at least from the pagan point of view.

The Ashanti priests receive no excessive remuneration for their services. Although there have traditionally been and currently are some few men who could be called unusually successful religious operators, most priests enjoy a comparatively moderate standard of living and depend for their basic incomes upon their cocoa farms. Few of them can support their families solely on their priestly incomes. Their fees are usually small—a chicken, three eggs, two shillings, occasionally a sheep—graduated in terms of the ability to pay and seldom so large as to work a hardship upon the giver.

In addition to the ancestors and the gods, the unseen supernatural is populated by a host of spirits, some helpful, some harmful, some just irritating—some all three, depending upon the circumstances. In the last-named class are the "little people," tiny imps or elves who can help the gods with their work, combat harmful spirits responsible for illness, steal palm wine, release an animal from a trap, twist a knife blade into the finger of a whittler, and perform a wide range of pleasant, funny, or annoying tricks.

Potentially or actually harmful spirits must be guarded against by charms specially designed to protect the owner. Many of these charms defend against sorcery, prevent ill-health or cure disease, ensnare a secret love or rekindle a dying passion, avert crop failure, or check the development of any of a large number of fear-creating crises which continually threaten to arise in a society which has inadequate control over the physical and social environment. Charms are similar to gods in their functions, except that they represent powers of an inferior order. They are constructed of ordinary or, sometimes, of exotic, mysterious materials which themselves possess no necessary, inherent power, but when mixed or brewed according to a secret ritual recipe by gods or mortals who have acquired the esoteric formula they are transformed into wonder-working objects. Their power derives ultimately from Nyame, who has created all things, and some charms, having proved themselves remarkably effective, come to have a personality of their own.

No society is without its mystical charms and magical nostrums, and those in Goaso are neither better nor worse than any others. None of them pass scientific tests of validity, but all of them make their users feel better, at least temporarily. They do what it is thought they do; if they do not, a friend can always suggest a better one that ought to be tried. The next one stands a good chance of success. The people of Goaso are certainly not morbidly preoccupied with problems arising either from fear or out of their unmastered environment. Their world is not populated by the threatening forces of unleashed evil. There are more than sufficient numbers of harmful spirits roving about in the world, to be sure, but they in turn are more than adequately compensated for by the still more numerous or more powerful beneficent spirits who desire nothing better than to heed the call of a good man and come to his aid. Sorcerers quake and evil spirits scurry for cover when all the forces of good are marshaled against them. The effect of this kind of world view is a clear reduction of anxiety.

The gods and townspeople of Goaso attend an orderly, well-managed religious service during the morning of the appointed day of worship, and Goaso's farmers are tucked quietly in their beds by nine o'clock at night. Private or semiprivate rituals enacted in a shadowy room lit only by a solitary flickering flame may inspire the uneasy sense of the presence of the occult, but these performances are really no more nor less awesome than a communion service by candlelight. Not only is the pagan public ceremony relatively sedate, but in Goaso, when the day of the god falls on Sunday, it is postponed until the afternoon so that the drums will not interfere with the 10:30 A.M. service in the Methodist church and the Mass in the Roman Catholic church.

In this tolerant, even cordial manner the Christian churches have been received in Goaso. During the thirty-two years since their introduction, membership in the two churches has increased slowly until now about one-third of the people are affiliated with them in one way or another. The Methodist church, established in 1925, has 50 members entitled to all the rites of the church and 75 associate members, who are not permitted to receive the sacrament of Holy Communion or Christian burial, but who have stated a desire to do so and are preparing for full membership. Nine adherents attend the ceremonies and activities of the church and contribute to its support but have broken some law of the church, most of them that forbidding polygamy. One hundred junior members, children enrolled in the Methodist school, complete the roster of the Methodist church.

The Roman Catholic church, established in Goaso in 1935, has four full members, 12 associate members, and 43 junior members, although many other school children and adults regularly attend its ceremonies.

The high proportion of school children in these statistics accurately reflects the major contribution of the Christian churches to Ashanti life—education. Each of the two churches in Goaso operates a school and each vigorously defends its right to do so even in a town as small as Goaso, for it is undoubtedly the school that is the lifeblood of the church. Although the churches do not finance the schools, which are almost completely subsidized by the Ghana government and by local taxes, the churches do provide the managing personnel and have trained many of the teachers. Indeed, Christians are frequently called the "schoolfo"—people of the school—and the church and school are almost always identified with each other. Because the yearning for education and the prestige and advantages it provides is so intense, it is perhaps surprising that not more people have become Christians, and it is probable that only the security and attractiveness of the old way of life inhibit more rapid Christianization, particularly in the rural areas.

If the school is a powerful inducement to conversion, it is not the only one. The following representative reasons for joining the church are supplied by local church catechists, trained laymen who direct the parishes in the absence of ordained clergymen.

"A man and his wife had been unsuccessful in their attempts to bear children; the gods to whom they appealed failed them, and they wished to try the Christian Nyame, whose desire and ability to answer prayers for children had gained some fame. Was it not true that Nyame had said 'Ask and ye shall receive'?"

"Some elderly people join in order that they may die as Christians, honored with the magnificent funeral the church provides, and able to face as Christians the ordeal of the judgment they have heard awaits them at death."

"A man and his wife joined the church because they were directed to do so in a dream in order to obtain the best possible protection against the sorcerers who were threatening them."

"While in jail a man heard other prisoners praying to Nyame and testifying that they were Christians; he felt 'the full weight of his sins' and wanted to confess and repent of them before Nyame."

"Young men and especially young women may desire to marry persons who happen to be members of the church, and they join in order to enhance their prospects."

"Parents and their children join in order to improve their chances for enrollment in the overcrowded schools."

That more people have not joined the church in full membership can also be attributed to two firm commitments on faith and morals which the churches have made: their ban on polygynous marriages and their prohibition of consultation with gods or other pagan agencies of protection against sorcery. A thoroughly Western interpretation of the Christian religion will grow only slowly because certain Christian beliefs run contrary to basic elements in the Ashanti world view. Many Goaso Christians will for a long time probably persist in having two souls instead of one, will regard their ancestors with reverence, will keep a wary eye on possible sorcerers, and will seek permission legitimately to enjoy their extra wives—if they can afford them—with deep self-satisfaction and thanks to Nyame, who so freely bestows his grace and love upon those who believe in him.

Church activities outside the schools are confined largely to services of worship, classes for religious instruction, and choir rehearsals. Medical and social services are provided mainly by the government, although the churches do participate in them to a small extent.

Conflict between denominations at the administrative level occurs mainly between the two major branches of the Christian church, Protestant and Roman Catholic, and between the larger and smaller, sectlike denominations of Protestantism. The Church of England, the Methodists, Presbyterians, and Baptists all appear to live quite peaceably with each other, more so at any rate than with the Seventh-day Adventists, the Pentecostal sects, and the Jehovah's Witnesses. By and large, the Ashanti seem little affected by these differences, for theological disputes are not their forte. On almost any Sunday in Goaso one of its wealthiest citizens may be seen walking from the Roman Catholic church after Mass up the hill to the Methodist church, whose service is scheduled at a later hour. He is frequently accompanied by several of his six wives—five of whom disqualify him from membership in either church, though not from attendance nor from contributing to their support—and by several of his more than twenty children, not including, of course, those of his sons who are currently studying in English and American universities.

This practical, ecumenical attitude well represents the feelings of most laymen toward denominationalism and, for that matter, toward pagan-Christian differences. Although most Christians assess their own denomination as at least slightly superior to others and regard their Christian beliefs as definitely superior to most aspects of the traditional Ashanti faith, in general they would sympathize with the sentiments of the pagan in Goaso who remarked philosophically, "Nyame is supreme. It was from him that the gods came. If someone wants to relate himself to Nyame in the Christian way, let him do so; that is his taste in religion. From the beginning the ancestors worshiped the gods. Now some people think they are civilized and attach themselves to Nyame. It is not my business to stop them. It does not matter to me that the churches oppose the gods. I shall stay with Bonsam and Nentiya. They are my legacy."

Both churches in Goaso are supervised by European missionaries, although the affairs of the local churches are conducted by African, professional lay catechists. A Dutch Roman Catholic priest visits his St. Anthony's parish for a day or two every six weeks to celebrate the Mass and to try to solve the perplexing and often frustrating problems of school and church. The Methodist church is directed by missionaries at much longer range and is visited less frequently, perhaps only once or twice a year. A resident Ashanti minister, however, is permanently stationed at a church just ten miles away, and he is available for guidance and for such special occasions as the funeral or wedding of a Christian.

The Christian church is certainly not a disruptive agency in Goaso or in Ashanti society. If there is any opposition to the church, it is expressed with little vehemence by those who quietly resent its cultural tone of voice—"they regard us as naked, lawless, barbaric children"—or its alliance with imperialism—"they gave us the Bible, and while we were reading it, they took away our land." Others criticize it for its modern political conservatism, allegedly fostered by missionaries as well as government officials as a calculated means of slowing progress toward self-government in Ghana. Many of these critics are part of a small but growing segment of Ashanti society which participates in the rituals of neither traditional gods nor modern churches, temporary agnostics who view themselves as too sophisticated for the old, too suspicious of the new, and rather hopeful that some satisfying religious amalgam can be compounded from the "better elements" of pagan values, Christian values, and science. The opposition to the church is neither intense nor bitter. Indeed, the church cannot be said to be under any attack; it is an accepted part of Ashanti life, ministering to the needs of a substantial minority who, for one reason or another, have found Christianity preferable to other forms of religious expression.

If Western Christians could not easily have foreseen all the reasons for the conversion of Africans to their religion, they still need not alter their belief that Christianity is an intensely practical religion. It is at least as practical as any religion, and, within their own systems of values, the Ashanti are as practical as any people. The church gives them something useful, even if the utility is not usually measured by theological yardsticks. Church membership may get the children admitted to school; the church helps many of those people of Goaso who have joined it to feel that they are safe from sorcery, that they will have children, that they will be kept in good health, that they will escape economic hardship, that they will have a splendid funeral. Others in Goaso, too thoroughly modern to fall prey to such "uncivilized" fears, find in the church a fairly satisfying attempt to fill the increasing religious void left by the accumulating disbelief in the traditional verities, the ancestors, the gods, the spirits of the unseen world, and all those mystical, supernatural causes of events.

Above all, the church has succeeded as well as it has because it is part of the larger Western culture, much of which the Ashanti want to appropriate for themselves. It is part of all those aspects of the Western way of life which have come to appeal to the people of Ashanti: schools and new occupations, travel and education abroad, national and international politics, science and medicine, roads and railroads and airplanes, politicians and lawyers and doctors and engineers and professors, new greater wealth and new avenues to prestige. The church by itself is not these things, nor does it necessarily espouse them. And yet it is a symbol of them that is within the grasp of anyone in any remote village who can never hope to possess the real things. He can become a Christian.

That only a third of his contemporaries in Goaso have become Christians reveals the tenacity of the traditional religion, and the satisfaction the Ashanti finds in it. The failure of so many to become Christians in spite of the gradual but irreversible decline of the cultural and intellectual conditions necessary for paganism also suggests the possibility of a modern irreligion. This alternative, however, seems too impractical, and therefore unlikely, for Ashanti. The remaining possibility is some still-to-be-achieved synthesis of Christianity and paganism, and this, of course, is the most practical and the most likely outcome for religion in Ghana.

10. The Future World

Most people are proud people. A society cannot long exist if most of its members do not take pride in each other and in the way their relationships are organized, if they are not convinced of the essential rightness, goodness, and worth of their way of life. This is one of the crucial assets of any living society of men; dying societies have lost their conviction or have had it crushed. For the dead societies only the historians, the anthropologists, or the antiquarians care at all, and they care only for specialized, unemotional reasons, because they themselves are members of another living society. Ashanti is a living society, and thus is not unique in its possession of pride. Its distinctiveness lies rather in the particular forms or patterns it has taken, and in these the pride of the Ashanti is justified even in the eyes of Western nations. That this is a significant justification is clear when it is remembered that these nations, compared with most other parts of Nyame's creation, not only are more proud of themselves but also have suffered more because of the forms their cultures have assumed and the pride their members have developed in them.

The best evidence for the strength of traditional Ashanti society and for the legitimacy of the pride the Ashanti take in it is to be found in their response during this century to rapidly changing social circumstances. Faced with the problems of living under a conqueror, however gentle in contrast to what might have been, pushed by superior alien forces sometimes direct and cruel, sometimes indirect and subtle, pulled by the attractions of certain obvious European technological and economic superiorities, persuaded of the superiority of certain social patterns, the Ashanti have resisted firmly where possible, yielded reluctantly where necessary, and grabbed eagerly where desirable. Not all changes, furthermore, are open to choice; many, perhaps most, just come inevitably with the others. But through it all the Ashanti have retained their identity and integrity as a functioning, satisfying society, without succumbing to the apathy of the hopelessly defeated, without abandoning themselves to a disorganized scramble for power by rapacious opportunists, and without turning their backs upon their past in order to embrace their present powerful, wealthy wooers.

The nature of Ashanti society and Ashanti pride in their culture is not solely responsible for the rather fortunate circumstances in which these people now find themselves. Inordinately proud people tend not to give sufficient credit where it is due, and the Ashanti, like the people of Western nations, tend to be inordinately proud of their own society. Those who are not may reflect upon the favorable natural environment which, unaided by the Ashanti, has performed a twofold service: presenting them with a setting rich enough in resources to support a sizable population and to afford a relatively prosperous economy, both before and after the Europeans came, and presenting the Europeans with a climate intemperate enough to inhibit large-scale immigration. Even now there are probably not more than eight thousand Europeans in Ghana, and few of these intend to remain permanently, a condition which contrasts strikingly with British East Africa, where many thousands have settled permanently, and South Africa, which has become a home to over two million Europeans.

Those Africans not too proud to be realistic may also reflect upon the nature of their British conquerors, who, whatever their reasons, harnessed Ghana with a yoke lighter and more helpful than that imposed upon almost any other colony in the world. Indeed, in many, though not all, respects their policies have not only eased the burdens of the colony but have reinforced and even restimulated Ashanti self-pride. If such reflections as these temper pride, they need not destroy it, for the basic facts of Ashanti social strength and adaptability remain.

The social reasons for Ashanti pride are shifting. Under the formal and informal pressures deliberately or incidentally applied by the British and the Western world in general to induce change in Ashanti society, some aspects of life have changed rapidly and drastically, others slowly and in small degree. Just how far-reaching will these changes finally be, and at what speed are they likely to occur? Such questions as these cannot really be answered; no one knows enough to answer them. The Ashanti do not live in simple isolation in a glass enclosure through which omnipotent observers can watch the changes as they occur. The Ashanti live in a world in which events far removed from them and having nothing directly to do with them affect what happens to them and how they respond to it. Few people would have been able to predict that World War II would propel the Ashanti and the rest of Ghana headlong up the road to full independence in little more than a decade. What would a third world war do? Few people, indeed, could predict what would be the

189

results in Ashanti of an economic depression in Europe and the United States.

Even without political or economic catastrophes—and these are only two obvious examples of an unknown number of events which might occur—highly specific predictions about future Ashanti society, or about any future society, are impossible. It is not that the Ashanti are any more unpredictable than other people; but unforeseen circumstances have a way of arising and human ingenuity has a way of devising or stumbling upon or falling into such a variety of action patterns that detailed blueprints are out of the question. Still, enough is known about human societies and about changes in their ways of life to permit some generalized answers to the question as to the future of Goaso.

Kojo Mensah, his nephews and sons, and probably many of the generations for whom Mensah and his relatives and friends will shortly become ancestors will remain farmers, for it is difficult to foresee in this area, or in most parts of the tropical world, any large-scale shift from an agricultural to an industrialized economy. There is little doubt that his success in the production of cash crops will support a standard of living superior to that which he now enjoys—which is itself considerably superior to that of his ancestors—but it will be perpetually lower than that of the industrialized areas of the world. From this there appears to be no escape, for Goaso's known natural resources are suited primarily to the feeding of stomachs, not of machines. The extraction of other resources such as timber or, perhaps, some yet-to-be discovered minerals may alter this picture slightly, but by and large Goaso will remain a homeland for farmers.

Indirectly Mensah may hope to benefit from planned industrialization in other parts of Ghana, such as in the southeastern region, where a near-billion-dollar project for the development of hydroelectric power and an aluminum industry on the Volta River are gradually proceeding toward actuality. The inevitable creation of some light industries and the establishment of processing or assembling branches of European and American industries also may increase Ghana's wealth and Mensah's market.

More directly, in a few years he may expect to light his home and run some of his tools with electric power, although intensive mechanization of his commercial farm is still out of sight. The availability of power and greatly improved communications by rail and road may even result in the establishment of small-scale light industry in his home town. The demands for consumption goods of European or American or, hopefully, Ghanian manufacture will rise steadily, and, if Goaso should succeed in becoming a transportation center for the Ahafo area, Mensah or his grown children and descendants may even consider a cautious venture into retail trade. Most of these new activities of significant size, however, will be financed by foreign capital, already deeply and solidly established in Ghana, and the prospects for local profit-making and intensive reinvestment appear limited. It is not, to be sure, impossible that Ghanians should rise to a position of economic dominance in their own country, but if they do, Kojo Mensah would do well to admit to some pleasant surprise as he pours a little Gordon's gin to his unexpectedly potent ancestors.

His future toasts, offerings, and prayers will more probably be confined to acknowledgment of the good sense which led him to add another cash crop, such as coffee or some other tropical agricultural product, to his production schedule. By so doing he can defend himself against the disaster of a prolonged drop in cocoa prices and against the loss of livelihood due to failure of the single crop. He should not expect to give thanks for any revolutionary economic windfall, for it is most likely that he and his descendants will continue to work their farms, agitate for higher prices, sell their produce to foreigners, and buy from them those goods which appear to make life more immediately enjoyable.

To do even this will require him to give some attention to a small but dark cloud on the horizon, for it carries the threat of land loss by small-scale farmers and increased tenant farming on large plantations owned by wealthy, distant, absentee, though African, landlords. Were Kojo Mensah a political economist he would look, if he could, for means to forestall this development, as the British have forestalled it until now, but he could not close his eyes to what he sees beginning to happen in other parts of Ashanti and the Gold Coast. He and those like him are still too close to the margin of profitable production, still not enough given to the careful planning of reinvestment to prevent their economic demise should events in world markets entirely beyond their control greatly reduce their income for more than a few years. Only a fortunate few can now afford temporary setbacks. Even their own mismanagement or bad luck in prosperous times places these little people in jeopardy to bigger people who have securely accumulated capital elsewhere and are only too happy to move in geometrically to increase their advantage. The sympathetic observer might hope for responsible government controls which will prevent any such large-scale developments. At the same time some production advantages would accrue from larger, more efficient land concentrations, and Mensah and the generation of his nephews might attempt to devise some means whereby they could retain control of their ancestral lands while pooling their production resources.

If the economic aspects of Kojo Mensah's future seem fairly distinct for the next few decades, the preview of his family life is rather hazy. So indistinct is it that it might have been well in the preceding paragraphs to suggest that, while Goaso's people will continue to be farmers, Kojo Mensah's nephews and sons may not be among them. For already there are visible signs of the disruption of family unity. And yet his matrilineal nephews and their nephews may still be working the land of his ancestors, for there are also numerous reminders of the stability of many of the old family patterns. These have managed to persist particularly because Mensah has been allowed to live where and as he does and to retain control of his precious land. Upon this factor hinges, in large part, the shape of the family to which he belongs by birth and that which he created by marriage.

There will undoubtedly be a continuation of changes already advanced in the modes of selection of leaders for family and community life. As Mensah grows older he will come more and more to realize that the once presumed wisdom of age and experience and the "natural" prerogatives of inherited succession to authority are no longer self-evident to those younger than he; he will see unhappily that leadership is veering away from him and his peers to the middle-aged or even to the young adults. In Goaso he will witness the rise to positions of leadership by those who are better educated, zealous for Goaso's progress, financially more successful, or politically allied with the party nationally in power. His nephews and sons may even outrank him in authority. But as he and the older men yield the positions once theirs by virtue of their age, inherited right, and at least minimum competence, he will realize sadly that his family and his town also must lose certain other of their once prized qualities.

The characteristics which now qualify younger men for leadership are characteristics for which the family has not been primarily responsible; they may be acquired apart from family membership. They represent a different kind of success from that automatically accruing to a person who has been born to the proper woman and has lived to a good age without obvious signs of mental, physical, or moral deterioration. Membership in a "good" family, whose members are sympathetic and co-operative, may contribute to the possibility of success, but this is no longer an absolutely essential contribution. Even though Kojo Mensah must endure the decline of his own position, he admits, however reluctantly, that there is merit in the change.

Once this distinction becomes widely understood and accepted, it will more than likely be followed by the gradual withering of the larger family groupings, the extended family and the lineage, as responsible organizations of supreme importance to the individual. If Mensah's nephews are numbered among the successful men of the future they will feel pressed to relinquish their interests and right to leadership in their extended families, because in a large family system the advantages of leadership are balanced by the disadvantages of obligations to support the less successful and dependent persons in the family. Mensah's recent ancestors regarded these obligations as privileges, perhaps worrisome and even irritating, but nonetheless essential duties of the offices of leadership. But then there were few open avenues to success outside the family. Now there are many more, and it is probable that fewer and fewer men will be willing to encumber themselves with obligations to their extended families. There remains a good chance that Mensah's extended family will retain at least a strong semblance of its old cohesiveness, but it will do so either because it has not produced successful men—after all, success, as the wider world reckons it, is available only to the relatively few—or because it is composed of the residue after the successful have sloughed off their family ties. Kojo Mensah, already nearing the twilight of his life, is probably safe enough, but the family security of his nephews and of their nephews is far more shaky.

As the effectiveness of the larger family groups diminishes, more and more of the burden of providing security and a focus of interest will fall upon the immediate family, parents and children, upon Kwami Bonsu, Mensah's nephew, his wife, and their sons and daughters. This, of course, is not a new group; it is a traditional group, but it will acquire new functions. In Bonsu's family the old social security patterns will be less secure, the feeling of dependence in emergencies upon a stable, willing, dependable kin group composed of Mensah, his brothers, and his matrilineal cousins less well founded. In it Bonsu can no longer expect gradually to yield his parental rights and obligations to his wife's brother, as he did in his traditional immediate family; he will retain these rights and obligations until death, and at his death he will want to bequeath them to his son. But will he be able to? The future is extremely misty at this point, perhaps because most Ashanti have great difficulty imagining a time when they would not belong to their mothers' families, would not inherit their property from their mothers' families, would not regard their sisters' children as their own, and would not have large matrilineal families to go home to. Or it may be that Kwami Bonsu can envisage such a situation but simply cannot perceive exactly how so radical a transformation in his society could occur. At any rate, he sees a swirling mist which could condense into any of a large variety of shapes, only one of which is now identifiable to any degree.

That shape is the looming hulk of litigation in the courts, as traditional custom and the functional demands of modern society clash for the next few generations to determine the structure of the emerging society. These conflicts arise in increasing numbers and scope especially in three crucial areas of life, succession to political power, control of landed property, and inheritance of wealth.

In the press for modernization and its benefits, both personal and social, aspirants to upward mobility, of whom Kwami Bonsu may well be regarded as representative, feel encouraged to assert claims to political power which, under traditional codes of eligibility, would have been summarily dismissed by one and all. Now a chief, traditionally elected, or a politician, secularly elected or appointed, must be nimble in deals and compromises if he wishes merely to maintain his position. The less agile can count on facing a succession of suits, any one of which or a combination of which may result in his downfall from office. Bonsu, automatically disqualified by his common birth for even hope of important traditional political offices, is coming to see himself in a new light, as more qualified than the inheritors of office by virtue of his superior education, youth, energy, and alignment with a potent national political party. While he may yet be unable to hope for actual accession to traditional office, he may nevertheless cast his lot in intrigue to supplant the incumbent with another member of royalty who has designs on the chiefship. And in modern Ashanti, with uncertainty infecting the old solidarity of the royal lineage, there are frequently several members of royalty working their way to the top through one means or another. In their success lies Bonsu's hope.

As land has become more productive of wealth in a cash-crop economy, its possession has become more desirable. Rights to use, once formally and informally acknowledged but unrecorded, now are brought into question, and the Ashanti courts hear the cases of individual versus individual and community versus community as they seek to establish their rights to land once free or to adjacent lands on either side of a once unimportant, widely acknowledged boundary line. Goaso itself has not yet enjoyed legal combat, but Mensah and Bonsu's friends in nearby towns have split into enemy camps over narrow strips of land and whole towns have accumulated staggering debts waging court battles over the wonderful trees.

Time and again, too, sons of fathers hopefully press claims against fathers' matrilineal families to acquire by inheritance what traditionally is not theirs but which in the new era they feel rightfully belongs to them. When a father like Kojo Mensah has worked land which he considers to be his own and outside the restrictions of family or community control, and especially when he himself has partially rejected— or at least considered the possibility of rejection—the concept of matrilineal obligations in favor of paternal obligations, the arguments wax warm. There is, after all, a great deal at stake in this comparatively prosperous region, and neither Kwami Bonsu, Mensah's nephew, nor Mensah's son can afford to yield the landed inheritance without a court struggle when there is uncertainty about the stability of the old inheritance code.

Uncertainty there is, increasing uncertainty, for it is doubtful that a modern social system can operate well under completely traditional Ashanti rules. The complicated functions of government demand persons with acquired skills rather than inherited prerogatives. Competition for wealth-producing property between individuals or communities which are becoming more estranged from each other, as the intimate ties and obligations of the old order loosen, requires sharp definitions of rights and boundaries. It is doubtful, too, that an inheritance system which disperses wealth broadly over the many members of a large family or lineage can successfully solve the problems of capital accumulation and concentrated investment.

The pressures for change are considerable, and they are reflected in the courts which—significantly for an understanding of this modern development—even in earlier times provided the arena for a favorite Ashanti activity, litigation, and a forum for a favorite Ashanti skill, eloquent oratory. Goaso is by no means rent with dissension; the traditions are here still holding their own. But the experience of more politically and economically significant areas in Ashanti indicates the direction of the future.

Were Nentiya and Bonsam to peer into the stone camera for a view of Goaso's religious future they would shudder just a little, for the gods are to be found only in the background. They are present, to be sure, and the tasks they once fulfilled so well are still being performed, but the gods are not so active as before. Older or disillusioned people may come occasionally and the older heads of the remaining extended families may beseech them desperately about the old days and how they might be sustained or revived. But there will be no reassuring answers, for none will be possible. Religious leadership will have passed to the Christian churches, whose schools especially prepared the way to near oblivion for the old beliefs. Perhaps the saddest thing to be seen is the demise of the ancestors, but then they appear to be too weak to sanction and control as once they did. Nentiya and Bonsam may be assured that the ancestors still live, to be joined at death by their descendants in Goaso, but in their eyes this will not be nearly so socially integrating nor personally satisfying as the old steadying belief that the ancestors are immediately with their children. Nentiya and Bonsam will still live, but few of Mensah's descendants will have much time for them, and Mensah himself will too quickly be forgotten by those who will have to learn about the once great ancestors through books.

Problems of health and disease will pass more and more out of the hands of gods and medico-religious practitioners into the laboratories and hospitals, where doctors and nurses have proved themselves far more effective. Problems of social control will slip away from the families and the local community into the hands of the state and the police, the courts and the politicians. Insurance against poverty—if not always effective and not always designed to favor the farmer as against the urban dweller—will be issued by the banks and the governmental agencies which control the currency, sell bonds, float loans, raise taxes, analyze markets, set crop quotas, experiment with diversified production and scientific farming, and manipulate a range of economic devices which the gods and ancestors never imagined were possible. The gods grieve, but they do not grieve unduly, over these changes, for do not the priests themselves benefit from these modern techniques? And cannot Nyame, the creator of all things, Ashanti or European, perform his works in many ways? Kwami Bonsu—comfortably retired on his Ghana government pension, pleasantly contemplating the safe arrival of a new grandson in the na-

199

tional hospital, and exaggeratedly recalling the exciting days of the great transition in which he grew up for the edification of his credulous grandchildren and a scattering of nephews and grand-nephews—will agree that Nyame can indeed work in many ways and that the later ones are probably the better ones, though he will not be completely sure.

The picture is not entirely bleak and discouraging for Goaso's gods, Nentiya and Bonsam. Christianity, as they foresee it, is not so radically different in any of its forms, and particularly in those more free forms which will develop in an independent Ghana. For the religious future includes the music of drums and dancing feet in an arena outside the church; the hymn tunes are Ashanti in their origin; it could be that the water of baptism is taken from the Tano River; the Christian ministers are still healing the sick miraculously and blessing the children and quieting fears with the promise of a great and good Nyame. The church members now and then call in the dark of night to appeal to the gods for charms, still suspect sorcerers of responsibility for misfortune, still remember and occasionally brew the formulas for mystical potions and construct magical devices. In some respects, it is even a heartening picture. In the cities, to be sure, many of the churches will resemble European churches very closely, and too many people in the cities and in the country will pay no attention to Nyame. But in the poorer parts of the cities—and these parts will be large and crowded—and in all parts of the country Nentiya and Bonsam can see much of their heritage continuing in clearly recognizable forms and principles regardless of the Christian garb in which they appear. And it will be an honest synthesis of honest religions.

Of all the pictures of the future, the political picture should be painted on a large canvas with a broad, vigorous stroke.

Journalists, propagandists, sentimentalists, and imperialists seem to enjoy doing this. But it is just this picture which requires the most cautious, hesitant treatment. There is so little tradition on which to base judgments, for empires have not been in the habit of granting their colonies independence, and those few which have received it have not yet enjoyed it long enough to supply the kinds and amounts of information which even a diviner ought to have. There is, furthermore, a tendency for these areas to acquire some of the outward symbols and institutions of the Western democracies that once controlled them without acquiring even the low degree of predictability of behavior which the better-known, better-analyzed democracies have.

Nevertheless, if the foregoing descriptions and predictions are valid, and if hope counts for anything, there is a strong possibility that a genuinely democratic political system in one form or another will be achieved in Ghana. There is the strong possibility, for example, that the Ashanti can permanently submerge enough of their pride and subordinate enough of their regional economic and political interests to participate in a representative, unified, parliamentary government with the other major areas of the nation. This form of government had already been developed under the British; for several years prior to the independence Ghana was governed under an elected, representative legislative body and prime minister, and its administrative posts were manned by Africans with the expert assistance of British colonial officers. Even now that the British have gone and Ghana is free to determine its own course, there remains the exciting possibility that a type of nationalist sentiment will arise which is moderate, realistic, and controlled enough to override ethnic and linguistic barriers with sufficient firmness to create a penetrating sense of political unity. If this is achieved, there will develop a kind of nationalism not founded upon the almost mystical attraction of a single, strong personality and leader, such as the present prime minister, Mr. Kwame Nkrumah, nor constructed upon now outworn, anti-British, anticolonial sentiments, but rising from the awareness of all the citizens that their security and well-being require a unified nation under responsible leaders widely recruited.

That this will actually occur in Goaso is far from certain. Instead, the scene for the next few decades is likely to be one of relatively little effective participation in national politics by people such as those living in Goaso. The old political habits and the old supernatural sanctions for government are disappearing, but only slowly are they being replaced by the new-style democratic habits and legal, secular sanctions free from emotional demagoguery. The pace of change has been much more rapid in the cities and among those relatively few persons for whom acquaintance with and acceptance of Western ways has been most effective and intense. But, living as they do in the country areas, Kwami Bonsu and Kojo Mensah will probably be manipulated from afar by regional pressure groups, by professional or occupational pressure groups, by the intelligentsia minority, by political parties which rise and fall meteorically over temporarily flaming issues, by a succession of strong men who leap to prominence only to slip from sight through their exploitable mistakes or corruption, by traditional, vested-interest groups seeking to reassert their crumbling authority. Mensah and Bonsu will be pulled this way and that by vote seekers, perhaps by authoritarian politicians who would prefer to abolish their ballots. They will argue, be argued at, be angry and uncertain. This is, in a sense, a kind of negative participation in national affairs, but as such it is hardly stable or satisfying participation. And the two of them and the others far out in Goaso will not count for much. On the other hand, they will be relatively free or will regard themselves as free to manage or mismanage their own affairs, and any Ashanti enjoys that feeling. Perhaps the most that can be hoped is that for a long enough time the people of Goaso can continue to learn, to argue, and to vote freely; that they will not be forced to suffer the painful social and personal consequences of violence and civil disorder; and that they can continue to enjoy an economy stable enough to assure them financial security and to support for several generations an educational program which will equip them to participate in the achievement of whatever political destiny they desire.

A composite of these predictive pictures clearly brings out certain general qualities all of them share. The people of Goaso, like those of all Ashanti, are changing their attitudes toward traditions and toward their historical past. Faced with a problem, Mensah and especially the younger Bonsu adopt a more rationalistic stance, within the limits of their ability, education, and motivation. They place less reliance upon the traditional solutions worked out by heavily religious or magical considerations; the past provides them with fewer clues to action, fewer hard facts logically discovered, fewer positive directives. And all the time the patterns, skills, and attitudes of the Western world become more attractive, more useful in the making of decisions. In the selection of leaders of economic or religious or political or other social action—or in self-promotion for such posts—Mensah and Bonsu place greater emphasis upon the possession of pertinent acquired abilities rather than upon the possession of inherited rights.

Not only are the rational qualifications for roles being more clearly stated, but the definitions of scope and quality of performance are becoming sharper, more coldly logical, more rigid.

But with these new characteristics to living there comes a change in the quality of the relationships between this man and his nephew, between them and their townsmen, between the people of Goaso and all the rest of Ashanti and Ghana. The old intimacies, the old sharing of ideals and plans and means of achieving them—or at least the understanding of them despite differences—the old regard for members of the families and the feeling that fellow community members are very nearly close kin, the old sense of assurance and of complete, immediate interdependence and mutual support are slowly disintegrating. Kwami Bonsu feels more and more that he must calculate his own advantages and strive for them even if it means intense competition with the very persons who formerly deserved the highest respect. No longer need he rigidly subordinate himself to his mother's brother, Kojo Mensah, to his family, to his lineage, or to Goaso; he may even be tempted to deny his responsibility to them, and they to him. It is up to him to make progress, and he cannot wait for the slow or lazy or sacrifice himself to help those who fail. Now he himself selects his associates, makes his own plans, devotes himself to whomever he wishes or to no one if he wishes, leaves home or stays, comes and goes, buys and sells, borrows or lends, recognizing only the authority of his own uncertain conscience, ignoring the authority of the groups into which he was born, counting his wealth in property rather than in persons.

On closer inspection this composite rather closely resembles a picture of human relationships in Western societies, and in a real sense it is in this direction that Ashanti society is tending. But the picture should not be interpreted literally. Goaso is not a European or American town, Ashanti is not a Western society, and the degree to which they possess the qualities of the described synthetic picture is not yet very great. In fact, not even European or American towns or societies conform precisely to this hypothetically constructed society, however closely some segments or aspects of them may resemble it. But Ashanti has moved in a westerly social direction and will continue to do so without ever becoming the West. Whatever it does become, its people will remain proud people.

Index

Accra, 24, 39, 130
Akan language, 21
Akim-Abuakwa, 130
Akim-Kotoku, 130
Africa, the bush, 6
  history, 13
  interest in, 5
  languages, 13
  literature, 13
  racial variations, 9
agriculture, 33, 133, 190
  crops, 15, 31, 34, 191
  instruction in, 82
  small-scale, 138-143, 192
  (see also Gardening)
Ahafo District, 30, 33, 111, 119, 191
ancestors, adjustment to change, 125
  demise of, 199
  influence of, 17, 154
  moral force of, 115
  remembrance of, 40-43
  reverence for, 161
  sickness caused by, 94
  social life, 160
Area Committee, 122
Asantehene, 107, 111, 123, 136
Asase Yaa, the Earth Mother, 140, 165

Ashanti (people), 8
  costumes, 150
  crafts, 148
  diseases among, 89, 90
  education (see separate item)
  family system (see family, the)
  future of, 199
  future social forms, 196
  home furnishings, 39
  home life, 36-43
  government, 18, 27
  language, 171
  leadership, 194
  life span, 87, 92
  make-up of, 30
  marriage (see separate item)
  medical theories, 88
  old age, 96
  opposition movement by, 130
  physical appearance, 8
  political power, 196
  pride of the, 187, 200
  religion, 154-186
  social problems, 44
  social structure, 187
  world view of the, 179
Ashanti (country), area, 28
  British colony, 104
  changes in, 98

Index

Ashanti (country), confederation
  (*see* Confederacy, Ashanti)
  democracy in, 104, 118
  education (*see* separate item)
  funerals and mourning, 100-103
  government, 18, 27
  land (*see* landownership)
  language, 21, 81
  monetary system, 131
  natural resources, 133
  political divisions, 21
  political future, 39
  political structure, 18, 104,
    105-109, 114
  population, 21, 30
  pre-British, 105-113, 123
  present-day, 105
  racial peace in, 22
  slavery, 18
  social classes, 123
  taxes, 109, 120
  topography, 7, 26
  transportation, 25, 35
  wealth, 53
  (*see also* West Africa)

Baptist Church, 182
beer, 148
Belgian Congo, 12
Bonsam, 166, 170-177, 198, 200
Bonsu, Kwami (a modern
  Ashanti), 195, 197, 199
brass, 15
British administration, 23, 29,
  104, 112, 118, 128, 135, 144,
  189
British Commonwealth of Nations, 7, 23, 39, 105
bronze, 15

capital, foreign, 191
cattle, 15, 133
charms, 178
children, 71, 73-86
  chores, 77
  discipline, 141
  games, 77
  heritage, 156
  infant mortality, 73, 87
Christians, 179
  leadership, 197
  theological disputes among, 182
Church of England, 182
clothes, 149
cocoa, 31, 34, 115, 121, 132, 134-
  146
  blight, 142
  co-operatives, 145
  farming, 79, 127, 131-153
  marketing, 143
  products, 134
coffee, 190
colonialism, 128
Columbia University, 78
communications, 191
Confederacy, Ashanti, 27-29, 123
  Council of the, 107-110
co-operatives, 145
courts, litigation in the, 196, 198
crafts, 148-150
credit, 132
crops, 15, 31, 34, 133, 138, 191

Dagomba, 130
Dahomey, 21
Dakar, 7
dances, 175
debt, 145
democracy, 84
  in Ashanti, 104, 118
  in Ghana, 201

democracy, old and new, 104-130
Denkyera, 111
diseases, 87, 90
  causes of, 91, 93
divorce, 58, 70, 115
dressmaking, 148, 150

East Africa, 7, 11, 22
education, 78-84, 123, 180
  curricula, 82, 83
  denominational schools, 84-86
  early Ashanti, 125-130
  prestige through, 126
  scholarship fund, 120
  teachers, 127
Education, Posts and Telegraphs, Department of, 32, 121
Egypt, 11
Elders, Council of, 99, 106, 107, 117, 119
England, 110
  Colonial Office, 114
  in West Africa, 105
  (*see also* British administration)
Ethiopia, 12

family, the, 16, 44-72, 97
  clan, 156
  close relatives, 49
  descent (*see* matrilineal descent *and* patrilineal descent)
  disruption of, 192, 204
  extended, 48, 104, 110, 195
  head of, 104-107
  leadership in, 51
  multiple wives, 46
  obligations to, 195
Fanti, 130
finances, 119-121, 131
food, canned, 134

Forest Negro, 8
France, 20, 110
free commoners, 124
French Equatorial Africa, 7
fruits, 15, 133, 138, 139
fufu, 67, 76, 163
funerals, 98-103, 159, 180
furniture, 152

Ga, 130
Gandhi, Mahatma, 82
gardening, 15, 133
Germany, 19, 110
Ghana, 7, 17
  area, 20
  birth of, 22
  British administration (*see* separate item)
  British departure, 112
  communications, 191
  democracy in, 201
  democratic background, 22
  development of, 190
  education (*see* separate item)
  geographical divisions, 20, 21
  independence, 19, 23, 153, 189, 201
  industrialization of, 190
  leaders, 22
  opportunities in, 22
  political organization, 20
  politics in, 119
  population, 20
  ports of entry, 24
  social life, 21
  transportation, 191
gin, sacramental, 43, 191
Goa River, 31
Goaso, 30-43
  agriculture (*see* separate item)
  annual budget, 119

Index

Goaso, appearance, 35
  architecture, 36
  civic improvements, 122
  climate, 33
  clothes, 150
  conquest of, 111
  education (*see* separate item)
  family system (*see* family, the)
  fighting men, 148
  funerals, 99
  furniture, 152
  future of, 190, 199, 202
  geographical location, 33
  government, 99
  headman, 114, 118, 123
  home life, 36-43
  importance of, 30
  incomes, 134, 153
  local gods, 166, 170-178
  markets, 131, 147, 152
  sports, 34
  wealth, 53
  Zongo quarter, 36
gods, 91, 163-186
  "little people," 178
  local, 167
  petitions to, 173
  representatives of the, 168
  sickness caused by the, 94
  works of the, 167
gold, 15
  workers in, 150
Gold Coast, British West Africa
  (*see* Ashanti *and* Ghana)
Great Britain (*see* England)
guilds, craft, 150

headman, community, 107-110, 113-119
health, 87, 90

holidays, personal, 140
Hwidiem, 35, 39

incomes, 134, 149, 153
Indirect Rule, 112
industrial development, 191
iron, 15
Ivory Coast, French West Africa, 19

Jehovah's Witnesses, 182

Kumasi, 28, 39, 104, 108, 111

labor, attitude toward, 141
  division of, 139
landownership, 135
  absentee landlordism, 137, 192
  individual, 137
  litigation about, 197
  traditional, 136-138
languages, 21, 81, 171
League of Nations, 20
Lever Brothers, 143
Liberia, 11, 25
Lincoln, Abraham, 82
liquors, 101, 148
livestock, 15, 76, 133
London, University of, 81

mahogany, 41
malaria, 89
Manchester textiles, 149
markets, 131, 147, 152
marriage, 54-64, 124
  basis for, 69
  boy's preparation for, 56
  bride wealth, 70
  Christian, 63
  conditions for, 58
  girl's preparation for, 55

marriage, multiple wives, 46
matrilineal descent, 46, 48, 54, 64, 74, 156
meat products, 133, 147
medicine, 75, 199
  mobile health unit, 95
  new methods, 95
  theories of, 88, 91, 94
medicine man, 92
Mensah, Kojo (farmer), 138-143, 156, 190
  future of, 193
Methodist Church, 31, 32, 179, 182
  missionaries, 32
  schools of, 79, 84, 85
milk, 76, 134
Mim, 36
missionaries, Christian, 32, 84, 183
money, 132
Moslems, 14, 36, 175, 177
music, 172

National Geographic, 31
nationalism, 129
Native Authority, 114, 118
Nentiya, 166, 170, 171, 198, 200
Nigeria, 21
Nkrumah, Kwame, 202
Nobekaw, 35
Nyame, the Supreme Creator, 23, 141, 155, 163, 200
Nzima, 130

old age, 96-100
oratory, 198
Oxford University, 78

patrilineal descent, 47, 48, 52, 74
Pentecostal sects, 182

polygyny, 16, 46, 63, 180
Presbyterian Church, 182
priests, Ashanti, 168, 177
Protestant denominations, 182

religion, 17, 154-186
  ceremonies, 172
  future of, 197, 200
  life after death, 159
  soul, 156
  spirit, 156
  theological disputes, 182
Roman Catholic Church, 31, 179, 182
  missionaries, 32
  schools of, 79, 84, 85
royal family, 107, 125, 126, 166

Sahara Desert, 11, 20
salt, 15
Sasabonsam, 166
savings, 144, 146
Sekondi-Takoradi, 24
Seventh-day Adventists, 182
sexual relations, 55, 56, 60, 70
slavery, 124
slave trade, 18, 109
social behavior, cause of illness, 93, 94
social security, 54, 97
sorcery, 91, 94, 179
Sudan, 15

tailoring, 150
Tallensi, 130
Tano River, 165, 200
taxes, 109, 120, 135
Te Kofi Nentiya (*see* Nentiya)
textiles, 149
Togoland, 19, 20
tools, 15

Index

trade, 148
transportation, 191
tsetse fly, 15, 76, 134
Twi language, 81, 171

Union of South Africa, 11, 22
United Africa Company, 143
United Nations, 20
University College of Ghana, 78, 81

vegetables, 15, 133, 138, 139

Wenchi, 130
West Africa, 8, 11, 104
    history, 15
    languages, 15

West Africa, natural resources, 15, 19
    peoples, 15
    political developments, 17
    political map, 18
    social classes, 17
    social life, 16
    topography, 7
    (see also Ashanti and Ghana)
wildlife, 133
witch doctor, 92
woman's status, 62, 64-72, 106, 139
    queen mother, 116
wood carving, 15, 151
World War I, 19
World War II, 20, 148

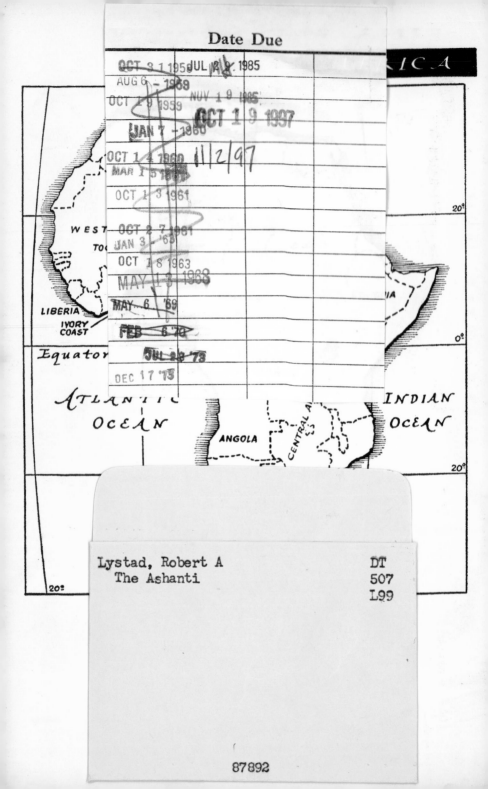